# Dedication

To my dear friend and pastor, Bob Yandian, who has personally invested himself into my life and ministry with absolute selflessness; to whom I am greatly indebted with the debt of love; who took the risk to believe in me and help thrust our ministry out into the nation in a greater way; and to the other men and women of God at Grace Fellowship, (Tulsa, Oklahoma) with whom I am grateful to be spiritually related.

# Contents

# Foreword

In my lifetime, I have seen tremendous progress made on the Church's awareness of spiritual warfare. Missionaries coming home from foreign soil would share how they came against the powers of darkness and won victories for Christ. Then I noticed skid row ministries and downtown missions preach on fighting the good fight of faith.

In the last twenty-five years, many intercessory groups have surfaced, all proclaiming total victory for the Christians and only by spiritual battles are spiritual victories won.

Rick Renner has done us a great service in writing this book. He has brought a truth forward for all believers. We are grateful for the insights given by foreign missionaries, downtown mission workers, personal workers, and intercessors. Now the time has arrived for all believers to "press the battle to the gate" (Isaiah 28:6).

*Living in the Combat Zone* is a manual for every believer everywhere for waging successful spiritual warfare against all the stratagems of our adversary, the devil. There are no pacifists in God's army. To be forewarned is to be forearmed. This book will show you the hows, whys, whens, wheres, and whos.

One source of personal joy to me is Rick's handling of Greek words. He is well-qualified to enlighten us with nuances, facets, shades of meaning, and further amplification of Greek words. I loved it when reading of Paul's dynamic conclusion of his life when writing to Timothy. It was deeply gratifying to read in Rick's paraphrase, "The good fight of faith, I have fought it. The course, I have finished it. The faith, I have kept it."

This is a book that you can use (1) before you start out to win victories for the Lord, (2) while you are in the midst of conflict, and (3) after the victory has been won. It is three-dimensional, and you will be a better Christian soldier from reading it.

Dick Mills

Dick Mills

## Chapter 1
# Living in the Combat Zone

If you've ever helped pioneer a new church, had a difficult role in leadership, stood with a cancer patient who was dying, gone through unbearable financial difficulties, realized someone was using you wrongfully, been taken advantage of, had to deal with a subverter, been deceived, rejected, and left alone — then *you have been in the combat zone!*

It is true that the front lines of battle are exciting. But it is also true that this is where satanic attacks are most frequent. It is here, on the front lines — on the cutting edge — where Satan hits hard and often, trying to drive back those brave fighters who are storming hell's gates in order to take new ground for the kingdom of God.

There is no place more exciting or more dangerous than the front lines of battle. *If you score a big victory here, you will be heralded as one of God's champions.*

However, if you are hit by one of Satan's attacks, it could remove you from the fight forever. Many great Christian leaders have been mortally wounded by the attacks of Satan. As First Timothy 1:19 says, "...which some having put away concerning faith have made *shipwreck.*" Recent years of scandal in the ministry have brought this reality painfully to bear on our minds.

To exist in the combat zone takes courage. It requires that you possess fierce determination, and it necessitates that you understand the strategies of the adversary.

Some in the combat zone become fatally wounded. Others become defectors, leaving those faithful ones still fighting with all their strength and giving their lives on the front lines.

Not wanting to keep up the fight in the midst of massive warfare, and fearful that they will be associated with radicals who might "fail," the defectors abandon the front lines of battle to which God has called them.

*God needs a special brand of believer who will challenge the foe and storm the gates of hell!*

God is still looking for those special believers who want to enter and live in *the combat zone.* While the risk here is certain, the rewards are the greatest. *When the battle is over, those brave fighters on the front lines have the "first pick" of the enemy's plunder!*

God is calling. He is looking for believers who will step forward to be counted. He is calling for those who will step ahead of the rest of the ranks and look the enemy directly in the face.

Are you one of these? *Are you called to live and fight in the combat zone?*

## The Place To Start

In studying about fighting, warfare, abandonment, defectors, and betrayers in the Body of Christ on the front lines of battle, there is no better place to start than First and Second Timothy.

Warfare in the Body of Christ today is nothing new! Actually, when you consider what the first century saints went through, our problems — which seem so large — begin to come into their proper perspective and are pale by comparison.

We see in First Timothy that things are going *wonderfully* in Timothy's first church. The church is growing. In fact, it is growing so fast that Timothy doesn't know how to organize it. In the midst of his church growth difficulties, he writes some questions to Paul. His church is growing so fast, he needs help from someone else.

From the content of First Timothy, it is obvious that Timothy is asking Paul about how to select leadership. He asks such questions as: "What about deacons? What about elders? What about women? How do I organize the Church?"

Paul answers all these questions in his first letter to Timothy. In short, he says, "Here are the qualifications for deacons; here are the qualifications for elders; here is what the women are supposed to do; here is how the young are supposed to act; here is how you are supposed to pay the pastors," and so forth.

*First Timothy is a book of instruction.* It tells how to organize a local church. The church Timothy was pastoring was in good shape at this time. It was experiencing supernatural growth; perhaps the fastest church growth of any in the first century.

## The Picture Changes

When we come to Second Timothy, however, the picture is very different. *In Second Timothy, we find that the church isn't doing well at all!* Things have changed. Timothy is fretful and worried. His elders are leaving him. His deacons are defecting. Persecution is at its highest ebb.

Not only is Timothy filled with anxiety over the declining condition of his church; he fears that he might be *martyred.* Rather than having a flourishing congregation, he finds himself leading a congregation that is shrinking. Things have definitely taken a turn for the worse in his church in Ephesus.

*Scandal, defection, liars, betrayers — all of these are problems which Timothy is now confronting on a daily basis. He has suddenly found himself in the combat zone!*

Timothy's predicament sounds similar to the condition of the Church today, doesn't it? In recent years, the church world and unbelievers have been *shocked* over and over again as major ministries have been caught in scandal. So many different stories are told about each scandal that no one knows who to believe. After a while, you begin to think they're all lying, and you wonder, "Can I believe anyone? Who's telling the truth?"

Then, to add more problems to this mess, financial indiscretions and moral failures emerge. Suddenly, it looks to a lost world like we *Charismatics* are all liars and immoral persons — money-hungry *scoundrels!*

## You Have Entered the Combat Zone!

Just as Timothy had to face daily problems of defectors, scandals, and betrayers, the contemporary church is now faced with the same problems. Times have changed for Spirit-filled people: We have left our "spiritual playground" of the '70s and '80s, and have now entered *the combat zone!*

The battle for souls, finances to spread the Gospel, the local church, and sound doctrine is growing greater every day. Our spiritual "la-la land" has disappeared, and the stark reality of warfare has been forced upon us, like it or not.

But what happened to throw Timothy into the combat zone? Something unexpected happened: *A demon-possessed man came to power in Rome!*

## Satan Personified

His name was Nero Claudius Caesar Drusus Germanicus. He lived from A.D. 37-68. Nero became emperor after Claudius I named him to be his successor. Nero promptly had Claudius killed and seized the throne!

*Nero was the first of ten very wicked, demonized emperors who reigned over the Roman Empire and hated Christians with a vengeance.*

First there was Nero, who was personally responsible for the deaths of Paul and Peter plus thousands of other Christians, A.D. 54; then came the horrible, miserable Domition, who exiled the Apostle John to Patmos, A.D. 81, and who made Nero's persecution look like a fairy tale for children by comparison; then Trajan, A.D. 98; then Hadrian, A.D. 117; Septimius Severus, A.D. 193; Maximin, A.D. 235; Decius, A.D. 249; Valerian, A.D. 254; Aurelian, A.D. 270; and, finally, Diocletian, A.D. 284.

Forced to live during the regimes of these pagan emperors, the Christians were hunted down like wild animals and were killed with a vicious hatred.

As we saw, the beginning of this persecution occurred under the reign of Nero, who was living at the time First and Second Timothy were written. *Nero's reign marked the beginning of horrible problems for all believers of that time.*

However, the seeds of demonic control began four emperors earlier, under the rule of Octavian.

## How Emperor Worship Began

Octavian came to power in 27 B.C. At this time, the religions of Rome were beginning to die and crumble. The educated had become skeptical concerning their religions, and had come to primarily recognize the ancestral gods simply out of respect for their past. It was a mere gesture of public relations designed for the older people.

Octavian, a deeply religious man who was immersed in pagan idolatry, was concerned that the empire was moving too far away from its religious roots. So he immediately began a campaign to revive the old Roman religions.

With the help of the Roman Senate, he rebuilt 82 temples of the Roman gods — at great expense. He removed all new religious literature that he deemed too advanced, and he returned the ancient, Roman sacred writings to the people en masse. He invaded the evolving Roman mind with paganism from the past, and it worked. These old religions began to become popular again.

But this was just the beginning of this new period of idolatry and paganism. After Octavian, Augustus came to rule in Rome. *It was with Augustus that the beginning of emperor worship began to take place.*

The Greek-speaking communities of the East, because of their deep, deep occult and religious roots, believed the reigning emperor was an incarnation of the supernatural and was worthy of godhead and worship. It was their strong desire to deify (i.e., make him "God") Augustus and even build altars and temples in his name.

Prior to this, during the revival of Roman gods under Octavian, a relatively *new god* emerged on the scene who would play a major role in *emperor worship.* This god was called Roma. This is important.

You may say, "With all their idols, gods, and images, why did the Romans need another?"

While there are several reasons, the primary reason was to unify the empire.

## Roman Paranoia Births a Monster

The Roman Empire was huge and diverse. At times it was so diverse that it almost seemed divided. Rome was a society that permitted nearly any religion to function (even Christianity in the earlier years was tolerated). It was a very free society, and Roman citizens enjoyed many rights. In respect to citizen rights, it was very similar to the United States of America.

In this tolerant climate, many religious sects developed, and different political factions emerged. Although the central government was strong, and citizens had many rights, the rulers, like the Russian communists today, had a paranoid fear of division. Therefore, they had to come up with a remedy to unify the empire.

*The god "Roma" was their solution.* By fabricating this spirit-god, the Roman rulers were bringing all the citizens in their far-flung empire to one point of agreement and unity.

Although the different religious sects and political factions argued among themselves, everyone had a great loyalty to the empire. They loved it; they had fought for it; and some of their loved ones had given their lives for it.

By fabricating Roma, the rulers of Rome were cleverly bringing all the people together on one major point: to give thanks to the "Roman spirit" for their powerful empire.

It was not long until temples were built in honor of *Roma.* Offerings were given to this pseudo-god. A priesthood was developed to serve those who worshipped in the temples of *Roma.* This was the god which all *good* Romans praised and worshipped. *This was a national religion and one national god which all could rally around.*

By the time of Octavian and Augustus, this *Roma* worship, a strange mixture of religion and politics, developed. It was this mixture that eventually started the terrible persecution of the Church. You say, "Why?"

Because *Roma* was recognized throughout the entire empire, and was seen as the great god of the state — the source of Rome's greatness and ongoing preservation — to reject *Roma* worship came to be equated with rejecting Rome herself.

*You see, Roma and Rome were interconnected.* In the minds of the people, they were one and the same. There would be no *Rome* without *Roma,* and the greatness of Rome could not continue without giving thanks to this great Roman god.

Because of this *Rome/Roma connection,* to deny *Roma,* or to refuse to worship her, came to be viewed as political rebellion.

"Why would you not worship our great state god," they would ask. "It is *Roma* who has made us great. Worship her! Do you mean you do not love Rome? If you love Rome, then you would worship her mother, *Roma!*" In the mind of the government and people, to deny *Roma* was the same as *denying Rome.*

## A Deadly Situation for the Church!

The people, recently invigorated by a revival of their religions, began to emit great religious power. They became controlled by this "god" and "gods" religion, and desired to see every part of life, society, and even government itself, controlled by a healthy respect and love for the gods.

Before Augustus, the new emperor, knew what was happening, the Greek-speaking communities of the East began to infiltrate the empire with seeds of mysticism, which eventually led to *emperor worship.*

The soil of the Roman heart was perfectly prepared by now to engage in a new type of idolatry. You see, idolatry never stays constant. It develops from one level of lostness to the next, the next, and the next. Paganism was now moving toward a terrible condition. That in time, produced a deadly situation for the Church.

The people gave the title "Lord" to Augustus. At this time in the eastern regions of the empire, the title "Lord" held all types of supernatural connotations. *To call someone "Lord" conferred deity and godhood upon that individual.* Augustus understood that willingly receiving the title "Lord" would make him *an object of worship.*

Like it or not, the people-at-large began to view Augustus as *the embodiment* of the Roman god, *Roma.* They believed Augustus was the *incarnation* of the supernatural — *God* in their midst. Because of this strong and ever-growing belief, they desired to build temples to him, sacrifice to him, and *worship him!*

## The Devil's Counterfeit

The devil always offers a counterfeit! At this very time, a *real incarnation of God,* the birth of the Lord Jesus Christ, would take place in Bethlehem! Satan was working to incarnate his demonic presence simultaneously with the incarnation of God in Jesus Christ!

At first, Augustus refused this deification. The burden of "being god" sounded too great. However, after a period of time, Augustus allowed this title to be applied to himself. And by 12 B.C., a huge altar, built by Drusus, had been erected for *the simultaneous worship of Roma and Augustus.* You see, by now there was no difference: *Roma was embodied in Augustus.* Suddenly he became more than a man in the Roman mind; *he was god!*

After Augustus died, Caius Caligula came to power in Rome. As the new emperor, he continued the tradition of emperor worship. In A.D. 40, he demanded a monument of Zeus to be built with his own facial features on the statue, and then he had it placed *in the temple in Jerusalem* to be worshipped, in addition to being worshipped in Rome!

After Caligula, Claudius came to power as the new emperor from A.D. 41-54. Although he never pursued worship and godhood, neither did he refuse it when he was called "our god Caesar!"

It was Claudius who appointed Nero to be his successor. Nero's insanity was evident almost immediately upon his becoming emperor. After being treated so royally by Claudius, once officially appointed emperor, Nero had him horribly slaughtered. This was just a foretaste of the terror that was to follow.

In time, this new religion began to take on a different form. *Since Roma was believed to be a national god, the source of Rome's greatness and preservation, to deny Roma was soon equated with denying Rome itself.*

## The Unexpected Happens

Their plan worked. This new idolatry soon began to unite the empire politically. The people quickly became consumed with this new god! *The common people began to regard the current, reigning emperor as the embodiment — the incarnation — of the god, Roma.*

*This emperor worship — one of the most deadly things that could have ever happened to the first century Church* — placed the Church in an awkward position. It eventually resulted in the vicious persecution of Christians.

On a large scale, it was this *demanded* emperor worship that brought about thousands upon thousands of believers suffering horrible deaths, becoming martyrs for the cause of Christ.

Believers would be brought before the proconsul of their geographic area. Standing under the shadow of the great Roman Seal, they were told to bow their knee, lower their head, renounce the Lordship of Jesus Christ, and pledge their allegiance to the deity of the current reigning emperor, who was supposed to be the divine incarnation of Roma.

When they refused, they were killed. *To say "No!" to the emperor's deity was to say "No!" to the god who had given Rome its greatness. This was viewed as an act of political rebellion.*

## Power-Crazed, Paranoid Nero

Persecution was especially brutal under Nero. Like all tyrants, Nero was consumed with power and was paranoid about subversion. He was indeed a madman, even executing members of his own family who didn't see exactly eye-to-eye with him on every issue. In addition to killing the majority of Roman senators and the whole order of knighthood in Rome, he executed his own mother, brother-in-law, sister, wife, and his dear teachers, Seneca and Lucian. He was more like a beast or a devil than he was a man.

While Nero first denied his desire to be worshipped, in time he embraced *his own divinity* and sought the worship of the empire. So obsessed was he with the notion of power, he went to the Roman Senate and asked for permission to tear down all the huge, beautiful buildings in the city of Rome.

Why? He wanted to rebuild them with his idolatrous statue in the center of every building. He wanted a symbol of himself in every major population center of Rome, so everyone could worship him.

In time, he had his way and built such a statue and placed it in front of his huge, new palace. It was a giant edifice, a representation of the sun-god — except for the fact that this idol bore all the facial resemblances of Nero: it looked exactly like Nero himself. With this idolatrous gesture, *Nero's insanity became even more blatant and his behavior more bizarre.*

(Out of this there emerged a segment of Romans who were so convinced of Nero's deity that for some time after he committed suicide, they believed in the second coming of Nero!)

## When the Senate Said "No!"

When the Roman Senate flatly refused Nero's request to raze Rome, tradition says Nero was so inflamed by this rejection that he went home, placed lighted torches in the hands of his servants, and told them, "If they won't let me tear down these buildings, then we'll burn them down!"

His servants were dispatched to every corner of Rome, and they began to burn down the city. The fire was so huge, it ravaged most major sections of Rome. It burned and burned. Some say Rome burned for more than a month. Out of 12 sections, only one section of Rome survived this terrible blaze.

In Nero's mind, this was "heaven." Now he could build *his* city the way *he* wanted it. Because he loved the arts and architecture, he saw this as his opportunity to make a permanent mark in history.

Naturally, you would think the biggest problem after the fire was all the huge, beautiful buildings that were destroyed. Of course, this was a problem, but not the biggest problem.

Rome had a minimum of 300,000 peasants and slaves who lived inside the city in little wooden shanties. When the fire consumed Rome, it also consumed all the homes of these peasants and slaves.

An easy solution to find housing for them would have been to send them elsewhere to live. However, these slaves were needed to rebuild eleven burned-down sections of Rome. Therefore, the Roman Senate had the tremendous job of finding a place for these 300,000 "homeless people" to live.

Realizing Nero had burned their beloved city, the senators lost all love for their emperor. They summoned Nero before the Senate, where he was to be *tried, convicted, and executed.*

On his way to the Senate, Nero had a diabolical idea: a plan to get him out of his dilemma. *He would blame the Christians for the fire!* He had a bone to pick with them, anyway. He hated them because they refused to renounce the Lordship of Jesus and call him "Lord"!

Nero was gleeful! His scheme was perfect! Christians did many things that he could twist and use to point his finger to their starting the fire.

## Why Blame Christians?

First, *in the Roman mind, a Christian was an atheist.* Because Christians didn't have any "god" that you could see with your eyes, Romans thought them to be "irreligious." Good Romans had all kinds of "gods" in their homes. There were statues and idols everywhere in their houses, so it was obvious that they were "religious." Christians, on the other hand, didn't have any kind of idol or statues in their homes. To the Roman mind, therefore, *Christians were atheists — without a god.*

Second, *Christians held illegal, private meetings.* In those days, unless you had the approval of the emperor, it was illegal to hold any type of meeting. Because paranoia was growing, the government had to know where the meeting was to be held, who was to speak, and what the intention of your gathering was. And if you met without this approval, they branded you illegal and *possibly* a subverter of the government.

Because Nero hated Christians, he never gave them approval to meet. Therefore, every time they had church, they were *breaking the law* and placing themselves in jeopardy!

Third, *Christians spoke of another king and another kingdom.* We understand they spoke of King Jesus and the kingdom of God. You must remember, however, that Nero had never given the Christians permission to meet in public, where they could have been overheard discussing these subjects. They were forced underground to hold *secret, private meetings.* Therefore, strange rumors began circulating about the Christians and their beliefs.

*In the Roman mind, and especially in Nero's paranoid mind, the Christians were planning the subversion of the Roman Empire. This was criminal! They were discussing a new kingdom and a new King!*

Fourth, *Christians held festivals called "love feasts."* We know what a "love feast" is: It is when you get together to enjoy a celebrative dinner with other saints and share the love of Jesus.

In the carnal Roman mind, however, a "love feast" sounded very much like a pagan orgy. *Thus, Christians were rumored to be highly immoral and possibly perverted! Sexual deviants!*

Fifth, take this one step further: *Christians had another ceremonial meeting when they experienced something called "Communion."* Rome had heard that the leader of the sect, Jesus of Nazareth, had said, "Except you eat my flesh and drink my blood, you have no part in me." *So it was rumored that Christians gathered privately to practice cannibalism — they were eating flesh and drinking blood!*

Sixth, the last charge leveled against Christians was the only accurate one. They really were doing this last thing. You see, Christians were standing on street corners preaching against sin. They were preaching about repentance and prophesying about the coming judgment of God. They were even preaching about *hell, fire, and brimstone.* They said a great judgment was on the way. They preached about the "fire" of hell.

*And, sure enough, the fire came!*

When Rome burned, people remembered the radical preaching of Christians! It was with this last allegation that Nero drove his spike into the coffins of believers everywhere. He convinced the Senate and people of Rome that it was these *atheistic subverters of government,* these *sexually immoral, cannibalistic, damnation-declarers* who had started the fire and burned down their beloved city. And the Romans believed him!

*That is when things began to change in Timothy's church and for believers around the world at that time.*

## The Early Church's Darkest Hour

Almost overnight, things changed radically in the Christian world. For a period of time, Christianity, like the other religions in Rome, had been tolerated. During this earlier period of toleration, the Church had grown, but now it was *no longer tolerated.*

In fact, if you were a Christian and were bold about your faith, you were hunted down like a wild animal and slain immediately — unless you were a citizen of Rome. Then you had to endure rigorous trials, long imprisonments, beatings and, finally, your final court appearance, trial, and sentencing. Your destiny had *already* been predetermined: DEATH!

It was in this hour of history — the darkest hour ever in the history of the Early Church — that the deranged Nero devised cruel ways to seize Christians and kill them. It would take a depraved, reprobate mind to come up with such horrible means of murder. This is why I saw he was more beast or devil than he was man.

Huge griddles were made on which they would fry Christians *alive.* Nero's entourage also developed the skill of taking knives and filleting the skin *off* believers in the same way one would skin a pig.

With muscles and veins, blood vessels, and arteries exposed, these Christians were thrown into heaps of manure. There many of them contracted diseases which caused them to die violent, spasmatic deaths as the diseases worked in their bodies.

Christians were forced to fight gladiators as "sport" in the Coliseum (which was against their beliefs). At times, they were wrapped in the skins of dead animals and thrown to lions. They also were made to fight to their death with wild beasts.

The devil was out to destroy Christianity then, as he is now. With these sick methods of death, Satan was trying to scare believers out of their Christian commitment.

The extent of Nero's slaughter can be seen by the fact that just one catacomb crypt found in Rome contained the skeletal remains of more than 350,000 people! Thus, millions of Christians died in the first century Roman Empire, just as more than six million Jews and other persecuted persons died in the Holocaust in the twentieth century Nazi Empire.

## Super, Supernatural Deaths

Tradition says Nero, now totally deranged and masochistic, came up with yet another sick invention — a huge slide. This slide was unlike the slide your children slide down. This entire slide was one huge blade, like a knife.

Believers were forced to climb to the top of the ladder, being ordered all the way, "Renounce Jesus Christ! Renounce Jesus Christ! Renounce Him and you can avoid this death!" When they refused, remaining faithful to the Lord, they were given a shove down the slide. By the time they reached the bottom, they were cut into two pieces.

Nero's backyard "garden" was famous. He had all the flowers and trees uprooted and removed. In their place he installed huge stakes that resembled sawed-off telephone poles. And in one area of his former garden Nero placed a vat filled to overflowing with hot tar.

Christians were brought into this garden and were forced to stand under Nero's balcony, where he could watch as they were commanded to renounce their faith. Those who refused were thrown into the boiling tar and then tied to a stake, where they were *burned alive.*

Nero was *determined* to get rid of Christians. Do you know why he wanted to do this? Because they called Jesus Christ Lord, and *Nero wanted them to call him Lord!* Satan has always been after the Lordship of Jesus Christ!

But look at the victory here! Some of the best historians tell us that as Nero sat at his window, smelling the burning, rotting flesh of the Christian martyrs, he was infuriated!

*He wanted to hear these Christians scream, cry, and shudder with pain as they burned. But instead of hearing them shriek with pain, cry for help, or moan and wail, he heard them...quoting the book of Psalms! He heard them...singing songs antiphonally unto God!* (An antiphonal song is a kind of chant. One person sings one part; then someone else sings another.)

Can you imagine? *Rather than moaning in pain, the Christian martyrs were singing together in other tongues as they burned to death!*

## The Real Battle Begins

Sad to say, not everyone was so bold. Some defected — *and this is where the real battle began.*

Yes, Nero was a problem, but his persecution was minor in comparison to the combat zone that emerged *inside* the Church.

For the first time, Timothy had to deal with *sabotage, betrayers, defectors, and deceivers.* The real battle was occurring within the walls of the Church, not in the pagan courts of Rome.

Some people said, "We'll see you later, Pastor. It's been fun, but we're going out of town for a while to wait for things to blow over. When things cool down a little, we'll be back." And that was the last Timothy saw of them. This devastated him.

*It is no different today.* People want to get in on a growing church until the devil hits it and things get a little tough, or until God requires something extra of them.

Then they say, "Well, wait a minute! I didn't realize this thing was so *serious.* I thought it was going to be *fun*!" And they "split." A fiery trial always reveals the real depth of people's commitment.

## Have You Ever Known a Defector?

Unfortunately, every church has experienced some type of defection. Nearly always, the defectors *claim* legitimate reasons for their departure. Maybe they disagree with the manner in which the offerings are taken, they don't like the last sermon the pastor preached, or they think the worship is too free. Most of these are *mere excuses* to cover up *a lack of commitment.*

Every pastor has had his heart broken, just like Timothy did, over people who leave the church. At least in Timothy's day, they were leaving for fear of being murdered! But if their desertion, for fear of being killed, was considered to be a lack of faith, then it is evident how *frivolous* most of our reasons are today.

There *are* valid reasons to leave a church. For instance, if doctrinal error is being taught, or if immoral practices are taking place or are condoned, you have valid reasons for departing.

Nevertheless, in the majority of cases, you discover uncommitted people using mere excuses that are disguised in a cloak of spirituality to avoid *responsibility.*

They may say, "I don't know why we're leaving. The Lord just told us to." Or, "We sense something is wrong here. We don't know what it is, but something is *off*."

I'll tell you what is "off" in the majority of these cases — those believers! *They view their drifting, uncommitted, carnal minds as the leading of the Spirit.*

These who depart so *easily* do not realize the seriousness of the battle, or the necessity of the local church. They may even claim membership in the *Universal* Church. Of course! That makes sense: If you're a member of the Universal Church, you don't have to participate in the *local* church! Isn't that right? No, that is wrong! The Universal Church will do nothing of consequence until it manifests in a local way — in a local church body.

Disagreements, trials, problems, and warfare always reveal the real commitment of people. Timothy's church was experiencing a defection because of persecution and imminent death. Regardless of these compelling reasons for defection, Christians are not called to defect; they are called to *stand!*

When you come to Second Timothy, you need to realize that this young minister was *overwhelmed* with the onslaught taking place to members of his own church! The battle has revealed their true colors — some by *deserting him,* are *deserting the church* and, more importantly, *deserting the Lord!*

## Advice for the Combat Zone

In the midst of this combat zone, Paul writes in Second Timothy 1:1,2, "Paul, an apostle of Jesus Christ by the will of God, according to the promise of life which is in Christ Jesus. To Timothy, my dearly beloved son; grace, mercy, and peace, from God the Father and Christ Jesus our Lord."

When writing here, Paul deviates from his normal salutation. In most epistles, Paul says, "Grace and peace be unto you. . . ." Here Paul says, "Grace, *and mercy,* and peace. . . ." This is very important. Paul inserts the word "mercy" in only three salutations in all of his epistles: in First and Second Timothy and in Titus.

Why? Because in all three cases, Paul is writing to someone who feels *overwhelmed* by his situation. For instance, in First Timothy, when Timothy had just assumed his leading role in Ephesus, Timothy is overwhelmed because his church is growing so fast he doesn't feel adequate to do the job.

Because of the awesome task at hand, he needs more than grace and peace; he needs to hear about God's *mercy* to help him in his situation! Have you ever felt such a need for God's mercy?

In Second Timothy, as we have seen, Timothy is overwhelmed because the church is *declining,* and because people are deserting him, the church, and the Lord. Now he is overwhelmed with feelings of hurt, rejection, and anger.

To continue his work in the Lord, he must have a special measure of God's *mercy.* Have you ever asked for a special measure of God's mercy to deal with a horrible predicament?

Imagine what Titus must have felt when Paul left him on the island of Crete to establish the church there. One of their own Cretian prophets had said, "The Cretians are always liars, evil beasts, slow bellies." Paul adds his own testimony by saying, "This witness is true" (Titus 1:12,13). Imagine trying to start a church with people like that!

Titus needed to know that a special measure of *mercy* was available to him for his difficult task. He needed *mercy* to work with the Cretians!

Isn't it good to know that when God calls you to do something difficult — something that overwhelms you — or something that you feel inadequate to do — He tucks a little extra mercy between the grace and the peace?

*There is a special measure of mercy to those who feel overwhelmed by their predicament.* This was especially good news for young Timothy.

It is good news for you, too, since you also live in the combat zone!

## Chapter 2

# Paul Reflects on Life as a Soldier

In Second Timothy 1:3,4, Paul writes, "I thank God, whom I serve from my forefathers with pure conscience, that without ceasing I have remembrance of thee in my prayers night and day; greatly desiring to see thee, being mindful of thy tears, that I may be filled with joy."

Make sure you understand the picture that is taking place here...

*Paul is sitting in a prison cell, being in a considerable predicament himself. In just a short time, soldiers will take him out on the Ostian Way, west of Rome, to behead him! In his hand he holds a letter he has just received from Timothy, his young son in the faith...*

As he reads Timothy's letter, Paul begins to reflect on all his years of ministry. Knowing he is about to depart this life, he can't help but reminisce about the past.

He remembers the high points and the low points. He remembers the good relationships and the relationships that went sour. There he sits, alone in a prison cell, with nothing but time on his hands — and now he holds a letter from the young man he reared and taught.

### Timothy's Troubles

His young disciple is in trouble. Terrified by his adversaries, Timothy is considering defecting and running away. Death could knock at any moment on Timothy's door, too.

In addition to this danger of martyrdom, Timothy's feelings are hurt, and his soul has been deeply wounded. He doesn't understand how his elders and deacons could stab him in the back and desert him after he has poured so much of his life into them. When he needed them, they were not there for him.

Rather than rebuking Timothy for struggling and being fearful, Paul writes, "I thank God. . . ." He knows Timothy's fears are temporary. But the primary reason Paul thanks God is because *he has already done his part in prayer* to ensure Timothy's success. "I thank God. . .that without ceasing I have remembrance of thee in my prayers night and day."

This word "remembrance" is extremely important. In Greek, it is the same root word for a "grave, tomb, sepulchre, statue, monument, or memorial."

You may ask, "What does *remembering* something have to do with a *grave, tomb, sepulchre, statue, monument, or memorial?"* The symbolism is significant. It tells us something about Paul's prayer life — and how he had been praying for Timothy.

First of all, this word "remembrance" refers to a grave, tomb, or sepulchre. What does a grave, tomb, or sepulchre have to do with remembering something? Or even more, *what do these burial words have to do with prayer?*

They tell us that before we can really begin to pray, it is necessary for us to dig through the current confusion of our lives and in our minds. Like dirt upon a grave, the clutter of life has a way of covering up things that used to be fresh in our minds. Especially today, when life seems to be getting busier all the time, it is not easy to pray. It requires a strong mental decision to discipline oneself and begin to pray.

By using this word "remembrance," Paul implies that he, too, has had to dig through some clutter in his life and make a decision to pray.

## The Time To Dig Deep

Paul has been through much hardship. His difficulties have exceeded any that we modern believers have experienced. Sitting there in his prison cell, it would have been possible for Paul to feel very alone, depressed, rejected, wounded, devastated, and forsaken.

Paul *could* have been destroyed — if by nothing else, by all the people he had discipled who left him in his hour of need. This alone was enough to destroy any man. (We must remember that although Paul was a great, legendary apostle, he also was a real man.)

Rather than being overwhelmed by all his problems, instead, *Paul has decided to remember.* Again, the Greek root for "remember" is the same root for a grave, tomb, or sepulchre. Now we come to the connection between these burial words and praying.

In order to pray powerfully, Paul knew he must put aside all his current troubles. Have you ever noticed when you're down in the dumps, it's hard to think about anything positive, or remember anything good that has happened to you? Flesh loves a pity party. Because of his many troubles, it would have been easy for Paul to hold a pity party!

Instead, he has decided *to remember* — to remember all the good things God has done. *He must dig deep* — beyond his current difficulties — back to other memories of good relationships and lasting fruit. Because his life has become so cluttered, this requires effort on his part. *He must unearth those memories, go back to where he left them, and take a good look at them.*

When hardship comes, and Satan attempts to discourage you, that is the time to dig deep. Stop where you are, speak to yourself, and *make the decision* to reflect upon the goodness of God.

You may have to take time to do this. You may have to enlist the help of other fighters in the combat zone to help you remember. I'll guarantee you, you won't remember by accident. You must *decide* to unearth those good memories, and brush off all the dirt. What strength will be imparted to you when you reflect on what God has done for you in the past!

## Comforted by Early Memories

As Paul looks back over the years, digging through all the rubble and trouble he has had in life, he comes to those early memories of Timothy! Suddenly, his heart softens, and he begins to thank God! "Ah! Here is one who has been completely faithful!" With thanksgiving flowing freely from his heart to God, now he is in the right attitude to pray.

When it seems everyone is forsaking you due to pressures beyond your control, and no one seems reliable, stop to think. *Look beyond your emotions and remember all the people God has brought into your life.* Name them one by one. Think of how you've seen them grow, and how much their friendship has meant to you. What satisfaction and thankfulness this will bring to your heart! You need to remember the good things!

*When thanksgiving is in the heart, it is easy to pray.* It is the clutter and busyness of life that makes prayer difficult. Get in an attitude of thankfulness, and prayer will come easy to you.

You ask, "All right, that explains those burial words. To pray, I've got to dig through life's clutter. Now, what about the rest of that Greek root — the words 'statue, memorial, and monument' — what do they have to do with prayer?"

By using this word "remembrance," Paul is saying, "Timothy, my intention is to pray, pray, pray, and pray for you until I have stacked the Throne Room of God with your name! *Anywhere God looks, I want him to see a living memorial of you!* I don't want God to ever forget you; therefore, *I am loading heaven with statues, monuments, and memorials of you. My prayers for you will stand as an everlasting memorial before God!"*

In fact, this same Greek word is properly translated in Acts 10:4, where the Word says, "...Thy prayers and thine alms are come up for a memorial before God." Prayers are living memorials before God!

Wouldn't you like to know someone was praying for you to this measure? Imagine the assurance it would give you to know a faithful friend was stacking the Throne Room of God with prayers on your behalf.

Many lives have been spared because of a mother or grandmother who prayed. Even long after they had died and gone to heaven, their prayers continued to exert power in life. Why? Because powerful prayers are permanent and everlasting. A prayer, prayed in faith, is never forgotten by God. It stands in His Presence as an everlasting memorial — like a huge edifice or marble statue!

I thank God for the partners of our ministry; for their offerings, of course, but also for *their prayers*. I want as many people as possible mentioning my name to the Father daily. I want heaven packed full of prayers — huge monuments — of me, my family, and ministry. Why? So God will never have an opportunity — not one — to go a day without recognizing our efforts to reach people.

This was wonderful news for Timothy — news he needed to hear.

## Never Forget What God Has Done!

Then, in verse 5 Paul continues: "When I call to remembrance the unfeigned faith that is in thee, which dwelt first in thy grandmother Lois, and thy mother Eunice; and I am persuaded that in thee also."

It's remarkable how quickly we forget God's faithfulness when we run into a problem. The problem seems so large and looms so lofty over us, we tend to forget that God brought us through the last problems. Yet time after time, God remains faithful.

This is precisely why Paul now begins mentioning Timothy's grandmother and mother. He is putting Timothy in remembrance of God's record.

It is almost as though Paul says, "You need to remember what God did for your grandmother! And do you remember how He has been faithful to your mother? God has never let you or your family down, so why are you worried now? God's faithfulness is part of your heritage!"

Often people with financial difficulties despair, not remembering how God got them through their last tight squeeze. And some people fret when they hear a relative or friend is extremely ill, forgetting that God has proven His faithfulness in the past by healing other loved ones.

Paul tells Timothy, "You need to stop thinking about the possible problems that could happen, and start remembering all that God has done for you in the past."

This is good advice to believers in any age. *Remembering God's faithfulness in the past will help you stay in the battle in the present!*

## The Real Problem: A Spirit of Fear

Paul continues, "Wherefore I put thee in remembrance that thou stir up the gift of God, which is in thee by the putting on of my hands. *For God hath not given us the spirit of fear; but of power, and of love, and of a sound mind*" (vv. 6,7).

What is Paul saying? "Times may be hard, but this is not the time to run. This is the time to stir yourself up for a fight. For God hath not given us the spirit of fear. . . ."

This Greek word "fear" tells us what Timothy's real problem was. His real problem wasn't hurt feelings. His real problem wasn't feelings of rejection. His real problem wasn't the elders or deacons who deserted him. No, these were simply manifestations of a deeper problem. Do you know what his real problem was? *Fear!*

The word "fear" in Greek is the word *deilia*, which always conveys the idea of "cowardice."

What do you suppose Timothy was *most* afraid of? Dying? No, it wasn't dying as a martyr, although that could possibly bring fear. Was he afraid of financial loss? No, material goods were not his cause for worry and fear.

Timothy was afraid that if he reached out to make new, close associates (e.g., new elders, deacons, new advisory board members, new staff personnel, and new close, ministry relationships), those new friends would hurt him the same way the others did. *He was most afraid of rejection!*

Like so many other pastors, he had poured his life into his deacons, *and they left him.* He poured his life into his elders, *and they left him.* And now he was faced with the process of selecting new leadership in order to fill the empty slots they left behind, *and he was terrified.*

He was saying to himself, "If I pour my life into these new people, what is my guarantee that they won't do the same thing to me that the others did? I'm scared."

Has someone you loved ever stabbed you in the back? This seems to be a common experience for fighters in the combat zone. When that happens, do you say to yourself, "Oh, well, that's all right; I'll just go make another friend"? No, you think twice before you commit yourself to that next person.

Back in the early days of our road ministry, a group of people said they wanted to pray for us. They wanted to host a regular prayer meeting in their home to pray for our ministry. We were thrilled!

Then I discovered that they weren't having us over to pray for our ministry; they merely saw us as a stepping stone to where *they* wanted to go. They were "using" us.

Hurt does not begin to describe what I felt; neither does anger. I was determined that no one would ever get close to me *again*! Often we are not aware when these feelings, these walls of protectionism, come over us. I was unaware of it, but subconsciously, I put up a wall to protect myself from ever being hurt again. I didn't even know the wall was up, but it was. You see, *I was afraid to trust.*

And this is what happened to Timothy — on a *massive* scale. He was afraid his new leaders would do the same thing to him the previous leaders had done. *This fear was immobilizing him!*

## The Things Christians Fear

If fear gets into your mind, you won't want to face anything; thus, it will produce *cowardice* in you. You will be afraid to get out of bed, afraid to go to work, afraid to make vital decisions, afraid of everything and everyone. If you allow it to do so, fear will eventually *control* your life.

Several years ago, I took a survey in all the churches I went to for meetings. I would mention certain things, and if the people had a fear of that particular thing in their life, I asked them to raise their hands.

*I was shocked to see so much fear in the Body of Christ:* fear of divorce, fear of cancer, fear of AIDS, fear of suicide, fear of insanity, fear of heights, fear of murder, fear of robbers, fear of attack, fear of financial failure, fear of demons, and so on.

*Those in the ministry had different fears:* fear of rejection, fear of failure, fear of lack of finances, fear of trusting people, fear of being left behind, and even fear of success!

If you don't regularly put God's Word into your mind, some stronghold of fear will get in there, and you will be overwhelmed. You won't even want to get out of bed to face the day. "You'll say, "Quick, someone — give me a sleeping pill!" You'll take it, say "good night," and as soon as you wake up, you'll reach for the bottle again.

This is why the Word says, "For God hath not given us the spirit of fear; but of power, and of love, and of *a sound mind.*"

Look specifically at that phrase "a sound mind." This is the Greek word *sophronismos* (so-phro-nis-mos). It is actually a compound word, the first part of the word meaning "salvation" or "deliverance," and the second part meaning "intelligence" or "the mind." When these two words are compounded together, they tell us something very important.

These words tell us what God gave us when we met Jesus Christ: He gave us *a new mind!* The Greek word for "sound mind" (sophronismos) literally refers to "a mind that is delivered or saved." I have jokingly called this "saved brains," or "a delivered head." But, in reality, this would be a very good translation.

The mind we received in the New Birth is supposed to be free from fear! It is "a delivered mind." It is "a saved brain." It should not be affected by fear and circumstances, for it has been delivered from such temporary fears and bondage.

Hebrews 1:15 says that Jesus came "to deliver them who through fear of death were all their life-time *subject to fear.*" This is part of our Christian heritage! Freedom from fear belongs to us! Jesus came to deliver us from fear! Instead, *Jesus gave us a sound mind — a mind that shouldn't know how to respond to fear!*

Your ability to walk in this sound mind is dependent upon you, just as it was dependent upon Timothy. You can easily submit to fear, or you can take Paul's advice in verse 6: ". . . stir up the gift of God, which is in thee. . . ." The choice is ours to make!

## Are You Fit for the Combat Zone?

In verse 8 Paul says, "Be not thou therefore ashamed of *the testimony of our Lord, nor of me his prisoner:* but be thou partaker of the afflictions of the gospel according to the power of God."

According to this verse, Timothy is tempted to be ashamed of two things: (1) *the testimony of the Lord,* and (2) *Paul, the prisoner of the Lord.*

Why do you suppose Timothy was becoming ashamed of the Lord or Paul? Simple: To maintain a solid, public witness for Jesus Christ was a deadly thing to do in those days. Because Paul hears fear in Timothy's letter, he encourages him not to defect on Jesus as others had. To make matters worse, Timothy is also tempted to forsake Paul, his own father in the faith. Why?

The great fire of Rome occurred in A.D. 64. In A.D. 63, one year earlier, Nero had released Paul from his first Roman imprisonment.

When the fire destroyed Rome, Nero proposed this theory: "I bet that fellow Paul was behind this fire! We never had any problems until he was freed. *That's it*! Paul, the leader of the Christian groups, planned and executed this arson!"

The fact that Paul had just been released and was living near Rome made him an easy target. Therefore, they tried to pin the whole mess on Paul, labeling him the *chief arsonist* of this fire.

Thus, to be identified with Paul was dangerous. To be his friend meant your name would probably be added to his list of accomplices. In light of this, Timothy was beginning to reevaluate his relationship with Paul! So Paul pleads, "Don't be ashamed of me, either!"

Paul had poured his entire life into the Church since his conversion, and now everyone was forsaking him. You talk about feeling *rejected*! And now Timothy is fearful and is considering abandoning Paul like the others.

Paul says, (1) Don't be ashamed of the testimony of the Lord; (2) Don't be ashamed of me; and (3) If you must, *be a partaker of the afflictions of the Gospel according to the power of God*.

## A Special Working of God's Power

What is verified in the Word and throughout history, is the inescapable fact that *persecution does come to believers.*

*However,* if those believers will stand true to the testimony of the Lord, *there is a special working of God's power for those believers.*

It was this special working of God's power that was in operation in Christians as they sang in tongues and quoted the Book of Psalms while they burned to death in Nero's garden. This is why Paul said, "...be thou partaker of the afflictions of the gospel *according to the power of God.*"

Indeed, there *is* a special manifestation of God's power reserved for those who suffer for the Gospel's sake. That is why First Peter 4:14 says, "If ye be reproached for the name of Christ, happy are ye; for the spirit of glory and of God resteth upon you; on their part he is evil spoken of, but on your part he is glorified."

God's glory and power always come to rest on those who are being persecuted or attacked.

## Paul Gives His Own Testimony

By the time we get to the Book of Second Timothy, Paul is no longer a young man. When he wrote this, his last epistle, he may have been 70 years old or older.

Paul was housed in a dingy dungeon, sitting in a cold cell that was slimy with infection and disease. He was all by himself, with the exception of Dr. Luke, one other faithful friend.

All of his other associates — those Paul had regarded as his best friends — had left the scene and disappeared when Paul was arrested. They left him like you would leave a house on fire: They got out of there! Even though everyone has left him, notice he is the one who is encouraging Timothy! Honestly, Timothy was in much better shape than Paul. Although many had left him, he still had friends and a congregation!

When he writes in verse 8, "...be a partaker of the afflictions of the Gospel, according to the power of God,"

Paul *knows* what he's talking about! He's been a partaker on all accounts!

To support his instruction to Timothy, Paul begins to tell his own amazing story of hard knocks. It is almost as though Paul wants Timothy to know he, too, has been through difficult times; therefore, he has a right to tell Timothy, "hang in there."

## The Rest of the Story...

Paul begins his testimony in Second Timothy 1:15 by saying, "This thou knowest, that all they which are in Asia Minor be turned away from me...."

Imagine if an entire geographical area rejected you? Yet Paul states, "...*all* they which are in Asia be turned away from me...." He was rejected by an entire continent!

When Denise and I first started our teaching ministry, we were traveling so much, we didn't know many people at home. We knew many people by face, but we didn't really have many close friends in Tulsa. Our close friends lived all across the United States, because at that time, we were only home about eight weeks out of the year.

There came a time when we needed to move from one house to another. I didn't know *one person* I could call on to help me move — not *one*! I thought about asking my father, but he had already helped me move so many times, I didn't feel I could ask him again. My brother-in-law was out of town. Other than my father or brother-in-law, I didn't know anyone well enough to ask for help.

My feelings were hurt, and my emotions began working overtime. I got mad at the entire population of Tulsa! Here I was, giving my life to God, and it seemed everyone turned away from me when I had a need! "Not one person in the entire city, which has a population of nearly half a million, would help me," I thought. I felt the whole city had turned away from me, and I began to throw a pity party.

When I went to church the next Sunday, I walked down the aisles looking at the people and thought, "Where were you when I moved the couch down the stairs by myself?"

I am not the only one who has ever had these kinds of irrational emotions! As irrational and nonsensical as these emotions are, we all experience them from time to time. It is ridiculous, isn't it?

And do you know why it is different if you are in a position of leadership? Because you pour your life into people all the time, and then when those people aren't there when you need them, ridiculous emotions try to make you feel hurt and rejected. *This doesn't mean such emotions are correct. Still, at the moment they are very real!*

Understand, Paul could have written the book on rejection! He had an entire geographical area turn away from him: *everyone in Asia Minor!* Think about how big that region is!

Then Paul mentions another very significant rejection. In addition to this rejection by the believers in Asia, there are two people he mentions by name who have caused him trouble. He says, "...of whom are Phygellus and Hermogenes" (v. 15).

Why are these two specifically mentioned? This was astonishing! Everyone knew that Phygellus and Hermogenes had been some of Paul's closest associates in Ephesus. In fact, some believe they were personally discipled by Paul, like Timothy was. Yet they forsook him! So Paul had been rejected by some very, very close friends.

Paul continues his testimony in verses 16 and 17: "The Lord give mercy unto the household of Onesiphorus; for he oft refreshed me, and was not ashamed of my chain: But, when he was in Rome, he sought me out very diligently, and found me."

Here it is almost as if Paul is saying, "Bless God, I do have one man who has been faithful to my friendship. Thank God for Onesiphorus."

Paul understands rejection. He has been forsaken by some of his closest friends and, even more, by all the churches in Asia. *Asia Minor is where Paul had done 90 percent of his work in the ministry!* This was an especially hard rejection to bear.

Like it or not, some people go AWOL in the midst of warfare. Even Paul had been shocked to discover many of his own friends had become guilty of desertion.

## Strong Warriors Remain Unaffected

Even so, Paul's attitude is still correct. He has not been affected by all this rejection. He is mad at no one. He holds a grudge against no one. In fact, all of this struggle and warfare — *living in the combat zone* — brought him to a place of fulfillment and gratification!

He says in Second Timothy 4:6,7, "For I am now ready to be offered, and the time of my departure is at hand. I have fought a good fight, I have finished my course, I have kept the faith."

Paul is facing death. He says, "...the time of my departure is at hand...." Yet, he is victorious! He continues to say, "I have fought a good fight...."

The word "fight" in Greek is from the word *agonidzo* (a-go-nid-zo). It is where we get the word "agony." By using this word, Paul tells us some of his ministry has been *pure agony; an unbelievable, almost unbearable contest* which we will study in detail further in this chapter. Yet Paul has not budged an inch! He has stayed in the fight and has been faithful to his call!

Really, the Greek sentence structure is reversed. It should say, "A GOOD FIGHT, I fought me one!" *The emphasis is laid on the FIGHT!* These are the sentiments of a man who has no regrets. He is proud of the contest he has been in. Regardless of all the others who have dropped out of the fight, Paul can say, *"I stayed in there. A GOOD FIGHT, that is what I fought!"*

Then he continues, "I have finished my course. . . ." This word "course" is actually the Greek word *dromos* (dro-mos), which always describes a foot race, or a running track.

Notice how Paul personalized this by saying "my course." He didn't attempt to run anyone else's course; he stayed right on track — true to the call which God gave him.

Although many others had fallen out of their race, and had cancelled their fight, he can victoriously state, *"Not me! I didn't fall out! I finished my assignment!"* Again, the Greek structure is reversed. A better translation would be: *"MY RACE, I completed it!"*

Then he says, "I have kept the faith." The Greek word for "kept" is the word *tereo* (te-reo). It conveys the idea of *remaining true to a commitment.* This places Paul far ahead of the rest of the gang, for many were not keeping the faith. They were letting it go in order to save their skin! But Paul can say, *"Not me! I kept it!"* Really, the Greek reverses the structure of this phrase. It says, "THE FAITH, I kept it!"

This soldier has everything to shout about! His ministry may have been difficult — and lived out in the combat zone — *but Paul made it!* He didn't give an inch to the enemy! And now, as he faces his own death, rather than being fearful, HE KNOWS HE HAS DONE WELL!

He says, "A GOOD FIGHT, I really fought me one! MY RACE, I ran it well and completed it! THE FAITH, I kept it and remained true to the call."

Then, rather than fearing death, he is really excited! In chapter 4, verse 8, he says, "Henceforth there is laid up for me a crown of righteousness, which the Lord, the righteous judge, shall give me at that day; and not to me only, but unto all them also that love his appearing."

Notice Paul says, "which the Lord, the righteous judge, shall give me *at that day. . . ." Paul knew his day was about there!*

Remember, in verse 6 he said, "For I am now ready *to be offered,* and the time of *my departure* is at hand." He could have been thinking about how they were going to kill him, what the blade would feel like, would he feel it at all, and so on. He could have been afraid.

Instead, Paul talks about "departing," not dying. He is ready to go. He is one soldier proud of the fight he has fought, the race he has run, and the faith he has kept! *No regrets!*

## Paul's Spiritual Combat Zone Story

Paul's story of hard knocks continues. Remember, he is not giving us this story in order to make Timothy feel sorry for him; he is building a foundation from which to speak.

When Paul tells Timothy to be strong in the midst of battle, he knows what he is talking about! He has been in the midst of battle himself.

When he speaks of discipling new men to replace those who abandoned Timothy, he has a right to give these instructions, for he has done this on numerous occasions.

When he tells Timothy not to give way to fear, he understands the temptation to fear. He has rebuked the gripping power of fear many times.

With this in mind, Paul continues his story of hard knocks — a spiritual combat zone story.

He says in verses 9-11, "Do thy diligence to come shortly unto me. For Demas hath forsaken me, having loved this present world, and is departed unto Thessalonica; Crescens to Galatia, Titus unto Dalmatia. Only Luke is with me. . . ."

*Now who was Demas?* Demas was noted among the apostles, and was very highly spoken of. For instance, in Colossians 4, he is mentioned right along with Onesimus (v. 9), who is called "a faithful and beloved brother"; Aristarchus (v. 10), who is called a "fellow-prisoner"; Marcus (v. 10), whom the saints are told to "receive"; Justus (v. 11), whom Paul calls "my fellow-worker" and a "comfort"; Epaphras (v. 12), who always labors fervently in prayers and has "a great zeal" for the saints (v. 13);

the saints (v. 13); then at last, *Demas is mentioned right in the same sentence with Luke.*

Verse 14 says, *"Luke, the beloved physician, and Demas, greet you."*

Demas was one of the leaders in the Church. This tells us that fear can affect any Christian if he or she allows it. With all his years of ministry behind him, and with all his powerful associates to lean on, Demas still gave way to fear and "departed" when things got too tough!

It's almost as though Paul says, *"You're not going to believe this one, son: Demas has left me!"*

Then Paul mentions Crescens and Titus by name. Why they left at this point we are not certain. Perhaps it was to take up ministry elsewhere. However, this left Paul in a very isolated condition, with only Dr. Luke remaining with him.

## Why Was Luke With Paul?

Here is one lasting relationship that Paul still has: Luke. It is a biblical, historical fact that everywhere Paul went, Luke went, too. This is the reason Luke could write the Book of Acts with such accuracy: He knew everything Paul did, because he went everywhere Paul went.

He even went to prison for periods, willingly, not having been arrested, in order that he might be close to Paul! *What a beautiful picture of covenant relationship this is!*

*Why did Luke stick so close to Paul's side?* Because, in the midst of all the persecution, Paul had been repeatedly beaten, and Luke accompanied him and treated him medically when he needed it, although he did not always need it.

We believe in divine healing and *know* that the Word teaches it. Praise God, based on Isaiah 53:5, we know it is God's will that we be healed *one hundred percent* of the time.

But have you ever run into a barbed wire fence and gouged your arm or hurt yourself badly? Instantly, you pray for your arm to be healed. However, if it is not instantly healed, you would naturally say to yourself, "I have to get something to get rid of this pain and stop this bleeding."

Paul had been repeatedly beaten. We know he had supernatural power flowing through him to heal his body, or his body could not have kept going. His persecution had been severe.

This is why he could write Romans 8:11, "But if the Spirit of him that raised up Jesus from the dead dwell in you, he that raised up Christ from the dead shall also quicken your mortal bodies by his Spirit that dwelleth in you." Paul knew first-hand of the Spirit's quickening power.

## The Intense Persecution Paul Faced

For an example of these persecutions, look at Second Corinthians 11:24,25. It says, "Of the Jews five times received I forty stripes save one. Thrice was I beaten with rods, once was I stoned, thrice I suffered shipwreck, a night and a day I have been in the deep."

Let's examine these persecutions one by one.

Paul begins in verse 24 by mentioning a severe punishment he had received from the Jews: "Of the Jews five times received I forty stripes save one."

This was not a beating with a bullwhip as most would suppose. *This was a special weapon of torture intended to teach its victim a lesson never to be forgotten.*

This whip was made of three separate straps of hide, one strap being made from calf hide, and the other two from the hide of a donkey. These three long straps were bound together at the base and tied to a very long handle.

At times, pieces of bone and glass were attached to the end of these straps in order to induce more pain and affliction upon the victim.

Rather than simply striking the victim, those carrying out the punishment were taught to hit hard, wrapping the three straps of hide around the victim's body.

Then, instead of letting the straps fall naturally to the ground off the victim, they quickly jerked this weapon — while the straps were still around the body — *hard enough to take off skin and leave horrible leather burns all over the body.*

If the straps had bones and glass attached to the end, these pieces of bone and glass would lodge in the skin. Then, when the straps were jerked back hard, *those pieces of bone and glass would tear out pieces of flesh.*

This sounds bad, but it gets worse. The victim had his clothes removed, and he was tied to two pillars, unable to move a hand to defend himself. *One-third of the stripes were given across the upper chest and face, and the last two-third were given across the back, while the victim bent over.*

At first, because Paul says, ". . .five times received I *forty stripes save one,*" it sounds like he was lashed thirty-nine times each time. You must remember, however, that *this whip had three separate straps.* Every time the victim was lashed, it actually laid three stripes across the person's body. Multiply this by thirty-nine, and you discover *each beating left 117 stripes on Paul's body.*

He says, ". . .five times received I forty stripes save one." Therefore, he has been through this grueling experience on five different occasions. *This amounts to 585 stripes across his body* — one-third on the front of his upper chest and face, and the rest on his lower back and legs.

## Did Paul Walk in Faith?

One man came to me in a meeting and said, "I guess Paul didn't know how to walk in faith. Had he known how to walk in faith, he wouldn't have gone through this ordeal."

The fact that Paul *could* go through this and still walk and function is the best evidence we have that he *did* walk in faith! He never gave in! The devil could not stop this soldier from fighting! It was his faith that carried him through! How would *you* fare in such a circumstance?

Then Paul goes on to immediately mention the next type of persecution he has experienced. In verse 25 he says, "Thrice was I beaten with rods. . . ."

*In the ancient world, this was a horrible, ugly form of torture which was regularly used.* Contrary to common belief, this was not simply the act of hitting someone with a stick. It was far worse than this!

A strong man would take the victim, bind his arms tightly around his body — very much as a straight-jacket would bind your arms. Then, with your upper chest and head lying face down on the ground, he would pull your legs up into the air.

Wrapping his strong arms firmly around your ankles, making certain your legs were restricted, he would expose the bottom of your feet to plain sight.

*At this point, a man with a huge rod, normally made of metal, would begin whacking the bottom of the victim's feet. He would whack, whack, whack, and whack until the feet of the victim were bleeding, broken, and maimed.*

At times, this beating was so harsh that the victim would never walk again. Hardly ever did the victim leave this beating without broken feet.

## Paul Escapes Being Maimed, Crushed

Once again, this tells us that God's power was available and was working in Paul. The fact that they did this to him three times tells us his feet kept getting healed! It would be safe to assume his feet had been broken three different times. Yet, *Paul still walks!*

As if this isn't enough, Paul goes on to mention his next memory of persecution. In verse 25 he says, "once was I stoned. . . ."

*The method of stoning was another vicious type of torture.* The victim was normally placed in the bottom of a pit, or at the bottom of a hill, with his hands and legs bound tightly. Standing around the rim of the pit, a crowd would gather above with stones (not pebbles!).

Then, at the same exact moment, they would all begin hurling their stones down upon the unfortunate victim, making his or her head their target. Often they hurled stones until the victim's head was completely crushed, assuring his death.

Paul testifies, "once was I stoned." It is generally believed that this was the same stoning mentioned in Acts 14:19. It says, "And there came thither certain Jews from Antioch and Iconium, who persuaded the people, and, having stoned Paul, drew him out of the city, supposing he had been dead."

*Paul's experience here was deadly.* Someone may say, "Doesn't this show a lack of faith?" No, it reveals great faith! Paul didn't *stay* dead! Acts 14:20 says, "Howbeit, as the disciples stood round about him, *he rose up*. . . ." From Paul's own testimony in Second Corinthians 11 and 12, we know he had died and been resurrected at least once in his ministry. This shows *tremendous* faith!

In Second Corinthians 11:25,26, Paul continues, ". . .I suffered shipwreck, a night and a day have I been in the deep; In journeyings often, in perils of waters, in perils of robbers, in perils by mine own countrymen, in perils by the heathen, in perils in the city, in perils in the wilderness, in perils in the sea, in perils among false brethren." The list goes on, and on, and on.

## The Beloved Physician

So to say Paul needed Dr. Luke's help from time to time, we are not negating the healing power of God! The Holy Spirit had quickened Paul's body on many occasions. Luke, however, was committed to be there to help out, if needed, *until* that healing power was manifested.

In addition to Luke, Second Timothy 4:19-21 tells us that four others in Rome had remained true to their relationship with Paul. He mentions them, saying, "Do thy diligence to come before winter. Eubulus greeteth thee and Prudens, and Linus, and Claudia, and all the brethren."

"All the brethren" refers to the church in Rome. These mentioned by name, Eubulus, Prudens, Linus, and Claudia, were probably leading members of that congregation who were not afraid to be closely associated with Paul. For them, Paul was grateful.

## Forsaken at the Worst Possible Moment

In Second Timothy 4:16, Paul goes on to describe another tragic moment of betrayal in his life. He says, "At my first answer no man stood with me, but all men forsook me: I pray God that it may not be laid to their charge."

The word "stood" is the Greek word *paregeneto* (pare-ge-ne-to). It is a technical term used to describe "a witness who stands forward in a court of law to support a prisoner."

By selecting this word, Paul makes his point clear: When he desperately needed the support of fellow believers, they were not willing to be associated with him. *He had been betrayed. No one stood forward to support him!*

In fact, Paul goes on to say, "but all men forsook me." The word "forsook" in Greek means "to leave in the lurch, or to leave at the worst possible moment." It conveys the idea of abandonment.

Paul keeps painting the picture clearer. He says, "Not only did they not come forward to support me and stand with me — they left me at the worst possible moment. They couldn't have picked a worse moment to do what they did."

## When the Lord Stands by You

You would think these horror stories would have made Paul bitter. But there is no bitterness in him. He has learned a marvelous secret: *If no one else will stand with you, the Lord will come forward to stand alongside you, support you, and help you.*

Continuing in verse 17, he says, "Notwithstanding the Lord stood with me, and strengthened me; that by me the preaching might be fully known, and that all the Gentiles might hear; and I was delivered out of the mouth of the lion."

Look at what the Lord did for him! First, Paul says, "the Lord stood with me...." This word "stood" in Greek is *paristemi* (pari-stemi), which means "to stand by one's side." By using this word, Paul tells us Jesus Christ is not ashamed of any faithful soldier. *If no one else will come to your aid, Jesus Christ will come to your rescue.*

Second, notice what Jesus did for Paul. Paul says, *"He strengthened me...."* The word "strengthened" in Greek is the word *endunameo* (en-du-na-meo), which always refers to "an empowerment or inner strengthening." It is where we get the word "endued." This is the very word Paul used in Second Timothy 2:1, when he tells Timothy to be "strong in the grace there is in Christ Jesus."

What was the result of all this? Paul says, "I was delivered out of the mouth of the lion."

## God Provides Angels for You

In the Lord Jesus' final hours in Gethsemane, He was nearly overwhelmed with His own feelings of infirmity. In this moment of need, He requested Peter, James, and John to go off with him for prayer.

Rarely, if ever, did Jesus need their assistance — they always needed His. But now, in this intense moment, Jesus asked them to pray with Him for just one hour.

Once, twice, He went back to speak with them. Rather than praying, there they were — sleeping — when He so desperately needed them!

Have you ever wondered where all your friends are, or were, when you needed them so badly? Jesus Himself was confronted with this same problem.

*Often it isn't that people don't care. They simply do not realize the greatness or heaviness of your burden. It is your burden, not theirs, and therefore they may not understand the seriousness of what you are feeling.*

At other times, there are those who just don't care. In the majority of cases, however, your friends are not fully aware of how great and heavy your burden is.

For the first time, Jesus needed His disciples to pray with Him, and they were asleep. He awoke them, but they fell asleep again.

## Intense Spiritual Warfare

In Luke 22:44, the Bible describes the mental and spiritual battle Jesus was experiencing: "And being in an agony he prayed more earnestly: and his sweat was as it were great drops of blood falling down to the ground."

Notice the word "agony." This is from the Greek word *agonidzo* (a-go-nid-zo), which always refers to "the most strenuous type of activity." In this case, the strenuous activity involved all of Jesus' spirit, soul, and body. He was in "an agony."

So intense was this "agony," that the Bible continues, "...he prayed more *earnestly*." "Earnestly" is the Greek word *ektenes* (ek-te-nes), which describes the condition of "a person totally stretched out." It is a word used to define the emotional condition of an individual.

This person is *stretched, expanded, and pushed to the limit.* He can't be stretched much more. In a certain way, he is *on the edge,* the brink, of all he can possibly endure.

Jesus' emotional state was so intense that it produced a medical condition in His physical body. Verse 44 says, "...and his sweat was as it were *great drops of blood* falling down to the ground."

"Great drops of blood" in Greek is the word *thrombos* (throm-bos), which refers to "thick clots of blood."

A recent study done by a leading medical school says Jesus experienced a medical condition called *hematidrosis* (hema-ti-drosis). This condition exists in those who are in a highly emotional state. The mind is placed under such heavy pressure and stress that it begins to send signals of pressure and stress throughout the body. So strong are these signals that the body begins to respond as if it were under real pressure.

The second layer of skin separates from the first, forming a vacuum. Blood quickly fills that vacuum, then begins oozing out of the pores of the skin.

*This tells us that intense spiritual warfare carries over into mental warfare.* This was probably the worst spiritual combat Jesus had ever been through in His humanity up to this time. And where were His disciples? Sleeping!

But here is the good news! Look at what it says in verse 43: "And there appeared an angel unto him from heaven, strengthening him."

When Jesus could find no one to stand with Him in His frightful hour of need and warfare, God provided! An angel appeared unto him from heaven, strengthening him.

*Regardless of your situation, your battle, or your particular combat zone, God will come to your assistance.* If no one else is faithful, God will abide faithful. Like Jesus Himself, who needed supernatural assistance, Paul was in the same predicament. And God provided.

Therefore, Paul continues in Second Timothy 4:17, "Notwithstanding the Lord stood with me, and strengthened me. . . ." So great an impact did this have upon Paul, he continues by saying, "And the Lord shall deliver me from every evil work, and will preserve me unto his heavenly kingdom: to whom be glory for ever and ever. Amen" (v. 18).

## Paul's Command

You say, "Rick, why did you go through this whole scenario?"

Because I want you to see that Paul was a man who had a platform from which to speak. He didn't just sit down one day and say, "Holy Spirit, let's write a little fun letter to Timothy."

Paul was speaking right out of his own life.

*He knew* what it meant to serve God on the front lines of battle.

*He knew* what it was like to pour life into someone, and then be rejected and forsaken by them.

*Paul understood life in the combat zone.*

*He had a right to speak!*

In Second Timothy 2:1, he says, "Thou therefore, my son, be strong in the grace that is in Christ Jesus."

This very, very important text is where we begin in the next chapter.

## Chapter 3
# Supernatural Power To Fight and Forgive

After living all of his life in the combat zone, suffering sabotage, rejection, defectors, and betrayers, Paul's attitude is still untainted with bitterness. He is excited about his remaining days, and he is thrilled at the prospect of seeing Jesus! He has maintained his victory in the midst of it all.

You may be asking, "How did he do it?" In Second Timothy 2:1, he says, "Thou therefore, my son, be strong in the grace that is in Christ Jesus."

This word "strong" is the Greek word *endunameo* (en-du-na-meo). This does not refer to toughness or macho-ism. Rather, the word *endunameo* refers to a supernatural touch from God — *an inner strengthening* that results from God's fresh touch in one's life.

It can also be translated "be empowered." This is a *supernatural empowerment,* and it shares the same Greek root for the word "endued," used by Jesus in Luke 24:49 to describe the baptism in the Holy Spirit: "And, behold, I send the promise of my Father upon you: but tarry ye in the city of Jerusalem until ye be *endued* with power from on high."

So the word "strong" (*endunameo*) refers to *a supernatural touch from God!*

## Moving Beyond Fear

In order for Timothy to move *beyond* his fear and his great sense of hurt because of those who left him, it is going to *require* a supernatural touch from God. Just telling him to change is not going to be enough this time. Timothy is so deeply imbedded in fear that only a supernatural touch will put him on his feet again.

*Are you ready to move beyond your fear?*

*Are you ready to trust people again?*

*Are you ready to step out with God and follow Him again?*

By using this word "strong" *(endunameo),* Paul is reminding Timothy that supernatural power was available to assist him during his crisis. *It is available to you, too.*

Timothy didn't need to face these terrible circumstances alone; neither should you face yours alone. God's power was available to give Timothy just what he needed: an inner strengthening — an empowering. If he would but reach out and take it, the power was available to Timothy.

It's available to *you,* too. You say, "Well, that is exactly what I need in my life! I've just come through a horrible church situation. I've been devastated by my ministry. People have left me. The finances fell through. Those I trusted stabbed me in the back.

"People I thought were my best friends are talking unfairly about me. My minister of music lied about me. My associate split the church. My friends have all forsaken me. My mother is still critically ill.

"I am *overwhelmed* with all these things! I am terrified! A spirit of fear is wrapping itself around me. You're right — I'm paralyzed with fear! *I need a supernatural touch from God!"*

## Are You Worthy To Receive From God?

You can be sure that, if you're living under fear, you're also living under condemnation. You won't feel "worthy" to receive a supernatural touch from God. You won't feel worthy to receive *anything* from God. You'll feel unspiritual, carnal, and defeated. You probably will have the overwhelming feeling that you're disappointing God. Have you ever felt this way?

You may think, "I know this fear is not God's will! With all my background in the Bible and the work of the Lord, I know this is *wrong.* How can someone like me — who knows God's Word — allow this to happen? God, please don't be disappointed with me for giving way to these feelings! Please forgive me!"

The truth is: *When you feel like you're disappointing God, you don't feel worthy to receive anything from Him.* You know what I'm talking about without my telling you. However, just for a moment, let's reflect on these horrible feelings of failure and defeat and unworthiness.

Have you ever felt so guilty about your walk with the Lord — so neglectful of it, or perhaps so powerless — that you felt too condemned to pray? You didn't even want to *look* at your Bible, let alone *read* it.

Really, it wasn't that you didn't *like* the Bible, or recognize your *need* for it; at that moment, you just didn't feel *clean enough* to read it.

You see, when you know that you're walking below God's will for your life, and you know you're not doing what you know to do, this always produces feelings of *failure* and *spiritual degeneration.* This is especially true if you are really trying to live for God, but you keep struggling with your predicament. What feelings of failure this produces!

In such a condition, you'll become so *self-condemned* that you may not even take your Bible out of the car after the Sunday service. You may sit in the car, look at your Bible, and think about how you should take it in the house and read it. Instead, you just leave it there.

You rationalize your actions by thinking, "At least I'll know where it is when I go back to church on Sunday night or midweek service." What judgment this brings to your heart, *knowing you used to read it every day*! Now you don't even bring it in the house!

Instead, you watch television night and day. You feel guilty about this, too. You know you could be using that time to be with the Lord. Then, when your children become ill, and a healing is needed, you feel totally powerless, and you don't feel like you have a right to pray!

## No Confidence in a Crisis

You may say to yourself, "I have no right to ask God for a miracle when He knows I've been avoiding Him." Because you feel like you've become a huge disappointment to God, you will have no confidence when a crisis comes and you need to pray.

Have you ever been there? Then you know from first-hand experience how horrible this backslidden, guilt-ridden, condemned condition is.

If this is you, you won't enjoy worship; you'll avoid conviction; you'll cease to pray in tongues; and you'll neglect your Bible.

All the while, you'll say to yourself, "I really need to change. I need to get out of this chair, turn the television off, get my Bible, and *change* what I'm doing!" Yet, no change occurs.

*Feelings of guilt and condemnation lock you into a state of stagnation.* You are in a fix, knowing you need to change, but feel too unworthy to ask God for His help. As one dear brother puts it, you are experiencing heavy-duty "condo-bondo" (condemnation and bondage).

At times, we have all gone through this horrible feeling of "condo-bondo" and degeneration. Thank God, it does not change the availability of God's power to help us in our need. Although such slothfulness is wrong (and you know it is without being told), be encouraged! God is still for you! This is when you need His power the most!

## Was God Disappointed With Timothy?

*This was probably Timothy's own spiritual condition.* Here he was, the leading elder and pastor of a once fabulous, but now degenerating church. He had been teaching his congregation the Word; he possessed deep spiritual revelation; he had traveled with the great Apostle Paul for years; he had seen God move, work miracles, and deliver them on numerous occasions. He had taught a great deal. He had seen a lot. And he knew a lot. *Timothy should have been a spiritual whiz!*

Yet, as Timothy observes the situation around him, he feels totally inadequate and powerless. He is walking far *below* what he knows. He has allowed fear to grip him. He has allowed feelings of anger and animosity to come into his life. He has contempt for leading members of his congregation who have deserted him at a very bad moment. All of these attitudes he *knows* are *wrong,* yet he feels them strongly!

Just like you and me, Timothy probably didn't feel *worthy* enough to ask God for a supernatural touch. Remember, in Second Timothy 1:8, Paul implied that *he was thinking about deserting the Lord!*

For this young preacher, who had seen so much, taught so much, and knew so much, to think about renouncing the whole Christian life and deserting the Lord, he must have been gripped with tremendous fear and hurt. *The combat zone had almost fatally wounded Timothy, and he was thinking about giving up.*

With all his knowledge, experience, and years in the ministry, he is living far below what he knows! Surely this must have produced a sense of failure in him. The great pastoral example was crashing — *right in front of everyone!*

He may have thought, "What right have I to ask God for help when I am failing Him at every turn? I am so self-condemned, I don't even want to talk to God. I'm not worthy."

## When We Need God's Grace

This is why Paul said, "Thou therefore, my son, be strong *in the grace* that is in Christ Jesus."

*The supernatural strengthening you need doesn't come because you deserve it.* If you wait until you *deserve* it, you will never receive one thing from God! It's just like salvation: "For by grace are ye saved through faith; and that not of yourselves: it is the gift of God" (Ephesians 2:8).

It is a religious spirit that tells us we must first become worthy *before* we can approach God. If you were *already* worthy, you wouldn't *need* to approach God!

Because you're *not* worthy, God makes His supernatural power available to you for *free!* Even when you are walking below what you know, God still makes His power *freely available.* This is why Paul says, ". . . be strong *in the grace* . . . ."

The phrase "in the grace" is very important. The word "in" used here is what we call "the instrumental case" in Greek. This means a better translation would be, ". . . be strong *by means* of the grace that is in Christ Jesus." God's grace makes this strength available to *every* Christian soldier!

This is good news! God's grace *never* runs out! As long as there is still grace, then there is still a free, supernatural, empowering, inner-strengthening available to you *if* you but reach out and take it.

If you are going to have the kind of strength the Word is describing, you must receive it *freely,* by means of God's grace. You are not going to have this power any other way. It is always — with not *one* exception — delivered to the saints "by means of grace." One expositor has translated the verse like this: "Thou therefore, my son, lay hold of a steady current of God's power which comes to you *as a result* of God's grace."

As long as God's grace is still in operation, a "steady current of God's power" is yours! God knows you need His power to fight in the combat zone. Therefore, He makes it available for free — just for the asking.

## If "Plan A" Fails, What About "Plan B"?

Notice when Timothy was in trouble, Paul didn't say, "Thou therefore, my son, go to Plan B," or "Thou therefore, my son, resign your church in Ephesus and put out your resume for another pastorate."

What does Paul say? *"Stay right there in the midst of your conflict and grab hold of God's power that is freely made available to you!"*

We must face the facts: *If God has called you to do anything — anything at all — there will be times when hell comes against you.* At such times, you may be tempted to say, "All right! I've had enough! God, You're going to have to pick another person to do this job, because I've had all I'm going to take!"

There may be times when you want to desert the original plan God gave you because it is *so hard* to fulfill. You may want to take Plan B or even Plan E. And if it isn't people hurting you, there will be something else to come against you. If it isn't a lack of money, it may be poor attendance in your church. If it isn't poor attendance, it may be a lack of communication. If it isn't a lack of communication, it may be an overwhelming sense of futility and fruitlessness. It it's none of these things, then it will be something else.

We *all* have opportunities and temptations to bail out! Sometimes those opportunities come on a daily basis, too! This is why we must learn how to open our hearts to God and allow Him to give us strength.

This supernatural strength *(endunameo)* will *empower* us to *stay* in the fight, to *keep running* the race, and to *hold onto* the call God first gave us. We must "lay hold of a steady current of God's power which comes to us as a result of God's grace"!

Regardless of the "why" of your struggle, or the depth of your present feelings of failure, you have only two options: (1) *resign spiritually,* or (2) *lay hold of a steady current of God's power.*

What are you going to do? Why don't you reach out and take hold of that power that transforms! It belongs to you!

## Extending Grace to Your Offenders

When my wife, Denise, and I first started our teaching ministry, we were deeply wronged by a local pastor. He had invited us to come hold seven meetings in four days, so we went. We poured our hearts out into those people. We taught with a strong anointing, and we saw many people receive immediate answers to life-long problems.

When the meeting was over, the pastor handed us our offering, and we realized he had *stolen* part of it. In fact, when I confronted him with this, he admitted it was true. He took part of the offering given to us to make his building payment.

I told him we *needed* that offering. His response was, "You're just going to have to trust God to meet that need." I was devastated! We had a $2,000 bill that was due the next day! I felt like I had been abused and betrayed!

The pastor had told the congregation that *every cent* of the offering was going to go to Renner Ministries. Not only had he deceived us, he had deceived his own congregation as well. I complained to the Lord, "If You knew this man was going to wrong us, why did You send us to his church?"

To make matters *worse,* our next meeting was suddenly cancelled. I was counting on that meeting to make up for what that pastor had done to us. Now what? According to our view of things, we were in deep financial distress.

I said, "Lord, what are we going to do? Our next meeting has been cancelled! If that man had not stolen our offering, we'd be all right. We're in a mess, Lord."

## "Return to the Scene of the Crime"

Do you know what the Lord told us? He said, "Rick, I want you to call that preacher who stole your offering and ask him if he would like to have you again this week."

I replied, "WHAT! You want me to go back there again? Lord, he's a deceiver! I don't want to minister with a crook! What if he does it to me again? Why would You send me back there?"

The Holy Spirit whispered to my heart, "I am sending you back because those people in that congregation have been abused and are dying for lack of spiritual meat. Obey Me, and I'll meet your need!"

Going back to that church was one of the hardest things I've ever done. I had to fight all kinds of emotions when I first saw the pastor again. I had to bite my lip to keep from telling him what I thought. I was there because the Lord had instructed us to be there — and for no other reason. I was there on orders from heaven!

In order for me to do this hard, hard ministry, I had to draw on that supernatural power Paul spoke of in Second Timothy 2:1, where he says, "be strong. . . ." Again, it is the Greek word *endunameo,* which *always refers to an inner strengthening or an empowering.* It is a supernatural deposit of power into the inner man.

With all the feelings of animosity I felt for that man, I knew I didn't deserve this power; I didn't deserve to be anointed that week in the pulpit. If I was going to receive this strength *(endunameo),* it had to come to me by means of God's grace!

Second Timothy 2:1 could be translated, "Be strengthened and empowered as God's grace amply provides all the power you need." I needed a lot of that!

Guess what? When that grace touched my heart and gave me the supernatural strength I needed, it did something else in me: *It made me want to extend grace to my offender!* With

God's power touching me so freely when I didn't *deserve* it, *how* could I hold any feelings of animosity toward this man who had wronged me?

When you have received the supernatural strength of Christ Jesus freely — without deserving it or earning it — it makes you want to walk in strong grace toward others!

## Are You Justified in Judging Your Offender?

If anyone had a right to hold a grudge, Timothy did. He felt forsaken, lied to, deceived, misled, and betrayed by many people. He had trusted those people! His feelings were very real. He had been deeply wounded. They really had wronged him! Instead of holding onto that grudge, however, the Word says, "be strong in *grace*. . . ."

When people hurt and devastate you, rather than judging them, *be strong in grace toward them.* Extend grace to them! And extend some more grace to them. And extend some more grace to them. And when you are through with that, you need to extend some more grace to them! "Be strong in *grace*. . . ."

*Extending grace does not mean to place yourself in a position to be hurt again.* It simply means to give them the grace that Jesus Christ gave to you: *forgive them.*

Think of the many times *you* have failed someone else, yet they forgave you. *You* may have been a betrayer at some past moment of your life. Have you? *You* may have misled someone in the past. Have you? *You* may have deeply hurt someone in the past, and even knew that you were doing it. Have you ever done that? Yet, when you asked God for forgiveness, He *freely* extended grace toward you! Not only that, those people forgave you, too!

When our wounds are fresh, we forget about all the deep wounds *we* have inflicted on others. A pharisaical spirit rises up within us; gooey sentiments of Christian love disappear, and a spirit of judgment and superiority begins to work in our hearts.

We may even rationalize that this time it is "different." But sin is sin; wrong is wrong. This is why Romans 15:7 says, "Wherefore receive ye one another, as Christ also received us to the glory of God."

The Word says we are to "receive" one another! And we are to do it in the same way Christ received us. How did He receive us? *Freely.* That is being "strong in grace." When we extend grace to one another in this manner, the Word says it brings glory to God: ". . .receive ye one another. . .to the glory of God."

Resentment brings no glory to God at all. It hurts *only you.* With all of the hard-hitting attacks of Satan from without, we surely do not need an attitude problem to corrupt and kill us from *within.*

While our brother or sister may have been used of Satan to hurt and wound us, the real sinister enemy is *not* them. It is the enemy working behind them, trying to sidetrack us; to get our attention on our wounds; to make us angry with others; to hold resentment and unforgiveness in our hearts; *to defeat us with a grudge.* Why give Satan this pleasure?

Remember, if you are deeply committed to the work of the Lord, you live your life in the *combat zone!* Every soldier, regardless of his human frailty, is important here.

If you are going to be victorious, or if you desire to be on the cutting edge of leadership, *of necessity* you must learn to see beyond the faults of others and learn how to extend grace. *Coping with human frailty is part of the Christian life.* Therefore, one thing you must do is: *"be strong in grace. . . ."*

### Getting Close to Other Combat Fighters

Paul continues speaking in Second Timothy 2:2. He says, "And the things that thou hast heard of me among many witnesses, the same commit thou to faithful men, who shall be able to teach others also."

Especially notice the phrase "the things that thou hast heard *of me. . . .*"

The word "of" in Greek is the word *para* (pa-ra). Literally, it means along, or alongside. However, it conveys more than this. It conveys the idea of partnership, a side-by-side relationship, and a very close relationship. It is the very same word used to describe the Holy Spirit in John 14:16,26; 15:26; and 16:7.

The Holy Spirit is called the *paraklete*, or "one who is called alongside" the believer. This means the Holy Spirit is our partner; He is side-by-side with us, and He is the closest of all friends. *No one is closer to you than the Holy Spirit.*

It is also from this root *para* that we get the word *parasite*. Again, it describes something that is "very close." You can't get much closer than a parasite!

Now Paul uses this word *para* to describe his relationship with Timothy in the past and present. Remember, Timothy and Paul had a long-standing, godly relationship. Timothy was not just someone who sat in the crowd and listened to Paul's sermon, taking notes. He had traveled with Paul. He had preached with Paul. He had worked the prayer line with Paul. (If Paul had sold tapes, he would have sold Paul's tapes!) Timothy did *everything* with Paul.

By using this word *para*, Paul confirms their close relationship. Verse two could be understood as, "The things that thou hast learned *by virtue of our close, long-standing relationship. . . .*" Or, "The things that thou hast learned *as a result of our side-by-side relationship.*" Or, "The things that thou hast learned *because I allowed you to become so close to my personal life. . . .*" These translations convey the right idea of the word *para*.

Paul is putting Timothy in remembrance of some early experiences they had together. It is almost as though Paul says, "Son, everything you know, you know because I allowed you to be *para* me — you learned by being *right next to my side!* You walked with me; you talked with me; you preached with me; you worked with me; you planned with me; you prayed with me. I did nearly everything with you, Timothy!"

The idea continues, "You didn't learn from me by just taking notes. You didn't learn from me by sitting in the back of the congregation. Timothy, you were right *next* to me. I let you *next to my heart* so I could teach you better. Timothy, you know me better than anyone else!"

This close relationship was the reason Paul could say, "But thou hast *fully known* my doctrine, manner of life, purpose, faith, longsuffering, charity, patience" (2 Timothy 3:10). Timothy was close enough to Paul to see all these things.

Now, back in chapter 2, Paul says, "And the things that thou hast learned *right next to me, by my side, by virtue of our close, intimate relationship. . . .*" (v. 2). He continues, "the same commit thou to faithful men, who shall be able to teach others also."

Notice the phrase "the same," because this is important. Paul makes his message to Timothy very clear after reminding Timothy of their close relationship. He says, "Timothy, you know what I have done for you. Now you get back out there and do *the same* for others. . . ." What does "the same" really mean?

This must have been terrifying for the young preacher. Remember, he has already chosen leadership once, and his congregation forsook him. He has already given his life to a group of people once, and he feels as if they stabbed him in the back.

If you have been badly burned by other people, it could be terrifying for you, too. To Timothy, this meant, get close to a *new* circle of leaders; get next to their side; share your life with them; walk with them; talk with them; fellowship with them, and so on.

## Commit Yourself to Someone!

Paul wastes no time before he makes his next command. Notice the next word Paul uses. He says, "...the same *commit thou*...." This word "commit" is also very important. It tells us what Timothy is *supposed* to do when he get next to the side of his new leaders.

The word "commit" is a Greek compound word, *paratithimi* (pa-ra-ti-thi-mi). *Para* is again the Greek word which speaks of relationship. The second part of the word, *tithimi,* means "to place, lay, or position something." When the two words are compounded, the word describes *the act of depositing something;* like depositing money into the bank.

How do you deposit money into the bank? You pull up alongside the bank depository box, open the drawer, place your money in the drawer, shut the door, and your deposit is sealed until you need it.

But Timothy probably thought, "Wait a minute! I already poured my life into one group of people. Then, when I needed them — when I needed to draw on that deposit — they were gone! My last deposit in people didn't work out too well. They hurt me. I don't know if I'm willing to make this kind of investment in people again."

This is taking it one step too far! It is all right to *walk in grace* toward each other. It is all right to *forgive* one another. However, does God expect you to *stick your neck out* all over again? That is *exactly* what Paul means! Stick your neck and your heart back out there and try again!

"In the same way I devoted my life to you, took risks to let you know me so intimately, and allowed you to understand me — *the same commit thou* to faithful men who shall be able to teach others also."

Timothy heard it like this: "I know those people hurt you, but it is not time to run. You've got to lay hold of God's power and do it again. You get out there and stick yourself right to the side of a new group of leaders.

"You walk with those men *the same way* I walked with you. Don't run away or let fear get hold of you. You must raise up some new leaders. Stick right by those people. Oh, and by the way, when you are alongside them *(para)*, pour your life into them *the same way* you put money into the bank. Walk with them and *deposit* your life into them!"

## Everyone Has Been "Burned"

You may ask, "How does all this apply to my life?" Everyone has been burned bad at least once in their life. If fear sets into your heart, you may step backward into isolation, never to develop relationships again.

If this occurs, you have been fatally wounded. *Satan's plan will have worked!* It is not possible for you to live and fight in this spiritual combat zone without the assistance of others!

You may have been hurt by a sister in the Lord; perhaps even a leading sister in the local church. Or maybe it was your best friend, a brother. You felt he betrayed you, or was two-faced, telling you one thing and someone else another.

Or perhaps you were not in the leadership of the church at all. Still, because you loved the church and were part of it from its inception, it has nearly killed you to see all the division and scandal that has taken place: elders disagreeing with pastors; pastors disagreeing with elders; and all sorts of other confusion.

This mess you've come through may have just about destroyed you. *What else can you do besides forgive them, extend grace to them, and start all over again?*

Any other option simply leads you into spiritual isolation and defeat. You have no other choice but to trust again. And yes, it is true, trusting again after being badly burned can be difficult. This, however, does not change the options.

If you have been wounded in the combat zone, it is time to be repaired and healed. Rather than allowing the wound to fester and get worse, you must trust God, stick your heart out there, and go for it again! What other choice do you have?

## Pick the Right Friends This Time

One of the reasons you have been hurt in relationships is because you let the *wrong* people get next to your side. It is a fact: This is the number one reason why people get hurt. It isn't because people get close to them; it is because *the wrong people* get close to them.

You say, "How do you know, Rick Renner?" Because I have done this a thousand times in the past. There is a strong mercy motive in my life. In the past, if you said you wanted to be my friend or be discipled by me, I would have said, "Great! Let's do it!"

Then I learned my lesson — the hard way!

I let people get close to me, and they discovered what I was *really* like. They were shocked because I didn't speak in tongues at every stoplight. They were shocked because I didn't immediately pray for the woman in the wheelchair in the restaurant. They became disappointed and disillusioned with me because I was a "normal" human being.

They thought, "He's a phony! He's different in the pulpit from the way he is in real life." Listen, saints, we are all human beings! My question for them is: Why weren't *they* praying in tongues at every stoplight. If they were so upset about the woman in the wheelchair, why didn't *they* pray for her?

Men of God are expected to be different. "Different" would be fine if that meant "holy." But in most cases, it isn't "holiness" they mean. "Different" to them means "abnormal, always supernatural, never natural."

For instance, we men and women of God are never supposed to use a road map; rather, we are supposed to be led supernaturally by the Holy Spirit. People expect us to say, "Yes, Lord. Yes, yes, yes. . . I understand! Turn right at the next corner, left at the next corner, go down three lights, and make a turn toward the south."

Likewise, men and woman of God aren't supposed to walk like other people walk. Instead, they are supposed to walk "in the Spirit." They are expecting us to do a constant "Holy Ghost Ballet," flitting here and there. They call this "walking in the Spirit."

As time goes on, we all learn the hard way to be very picky about *who* gets next to our side. While you should not judge or be suspicious about people, it is essential that you have people next to your side whom you can trust and relate to. *You need people with enough spiritual maturity to understand you are a normal person as well as a Spirit-filled combat fighter.* A human being!

Paul seems to say, "Timothy, the problem is not people. The problem is you made elders and deacons out of the *wrong* people!" Maybe Timothy had previously checked their affluence in the community; maybe he had been influenced by their wealth. It would naturally make sense to put someone with a lot of money into leadership, right? Just think of all the help and advice this person could give, right?

No! Unless the person is filled with the Holy Spirit, you don't want him or her in a position of leadership.

*Who* you allow next to your side is very important. Remember, you are placing a deposit of your own life into them. That deposit is precious. While you do not want to be suspicious, neither do you want to make a stupid mistake that will eventually wound you. The battle you're fighting is fierce enough without your adding more problems to it. Make certain you have the right person (or people) to entrust yourself to the next time!

## The Best Fighters: "Faithful Men"

Do you know who Timothy *should* have picked for elders and deacons? The people who hung around when everyone else left! These should have been his leadership.

Those who stayed were probably not as influential as the others. All he had left were "regular" people: janitors, garbage collectors, mechanics, and so on. All the "spiritual giants" were gone. Now all he had were those who set up chairs for the service, the greeters, ushers, and "support" ministry. When everyone else left, they stayed true.

Don't you thank God for all your friends who have remained true through the years? Early in your life, you think friends come a dime a dozen. However, as life goes on, and you begin to mature, you realize the list of your genuine friends gets smaller and smaller.

There are several reasons for this: Life gets busy, people move from one city to another, jobs change, people change churches, and so on. The friendships that endure it all are *precious gifts!* Thank God for a real friend who is "faithful" through it all!

## "Faithful Men" Commended

This is why Paul said, "And the things that thou hast heard of me. . .the same commit thou to *faithful men,* who shall be able to teach others also."

Timothy understood Paul's message. He knew Paul meant, "The things that you heard from me while you were next to my side, get out there and do for others! You must affix your life to a new group of people. However, this time pick the right people. Make sure you entrust yourself to *faithful men!*" Faithful men!

Now let's clarify something here: Paul is emphasizing faithfulness, *not* ability. He didn't say, "Look for qualified men." I'll tell you, there are many qualified people that you don't want doing the job.

There are many, many qualified people who can direct music, but you might end up thinking the devil himself has fallen right into your church choir loft because of competition between the music director and the pastor!

Don't leap just because someone *says* he is skilled. Don't *quickly* commit yourself to someone just because he impresses you!

The Bible says in First Timothy 5:22, "Lay hands suddenly on no man, neither be partaker of other men's sins: keep thyself pure." This scripture is teaching us to be careful.

Furthermore, don't lay hands on people just because they were used to a great degree in the last church. Wait until you know them. *Then* lay hands on them.

If you lay hands on them prematurely, only to discover their heart is not right with God (perhaps they are stubborn and hard to deal with), to a degree you're going to become a "partaker of other men's sins." You'll have to deal with the mess. That is why Paul continued to say, "keep thyself pure." Know the person before you lay hands on him!

Likewise, make sure you can really trust someone before you commit the deep, dark secrets of your life to him. Many innocent Christians have been wounded because they shared something private with a person who was not mature enough to handle it. Then, to their dismay, they discovered the whole church knew about it.

More than that, the person whom they trusted was so turned off by what they confided, they rejected their friendship! This hurts the heart! This is why Paul emphasizes "faithful men."

Understand that it is good if you can find a qualified person, but Paul says to look for "faithful men." If you can find a faithful person who is also qualified, you've come across a real gem! Faithfulness, however, is what we should really seek.

There are many people who can handle money wisely, but they are not necessarily the right people to put in charge of the church treasury. They may just step into that position and try to take over! They may want to *control* every penny and *correct* the leadership every time the leadership wants to do something.

If you choose someone too hastily for a position, you're probably going to end up praying that person out of the position — and hoping it can be done without causing a church rift!

If you're a pastor, make sure you pick the right people for your advisory board, or their position may go to their head! They may end up wanting to tell you what to preach and what not to preach. *Look for faithfulness!*

Perhaps you're saying, "What about me? I'm not in the ministry. Does this apply to me, too?" Yes, it applies to *all* of us.

While we are brothers and sisters who will spend eternity together regardless of what we *do* to each other here, we must make wise choices when we choose close friends. Otherwise, hurts and wounds are going to be laid upon our hearts, temporarily or maybe permanently, removing us from the battle we need to be fighting.

## Faithfulness in Three Areas

When discussing faithfulness, three primary areas of faithfulness are a "must." They are: (1) *faithfulness to God,* (2) *faithfulness to relationships,* and (3) *faithfulness in activities or service.* These three areas of faithfulness are vital.

The first area is *faithfulness to God.* Really, this needs no great explanation. We know that we are to be faithful to God. If we are genuinely faithful to God, however, it will manifest in the next two areas.

The second area is *faithfulness to relationships.* This is an area of faithfulness that people (especially Charismatics) need to work on diligently! Remember, this is where Timothy had made his mistake! He chose people who were possibly qualified and influential, but *unfaithful.* When he needed them, they said, "See you later!"

*Before God is going to entrust great responsibility to you in the local church, He first will wait on you to see if you can remain faithful to your relationship with your pastor and your local church.*

Honestly, if you cannot let a "man of God" also be a "man," then you do not deserve a place of leadership next to him.

If you are not committed enough to believe he is anointed, even when you see him struggle, then you should not be in leadership. People are people, and pastors (or those in authority) need faithful people around them; people who will see *beyond* their faults and *still respect their leadership.*

Faithfulness to relationships is an absolute *must* to be used of God! Remember, we're combat zone believers! When the enemy's missiles are flying all around, at times the flesh reacts wrong. My, how those missiles have a way of stirring up rank, ugly flesh. It happens to everyone. Will you remain faithful to that relationship regardless?

The third area of faithfulness is *faithfulness in activities or service in the work of the Lord.* In other words, learning to be a servant; doing what you're asked to do, when you're asked to do it, even when your flesh rises up in disgust.

God entrusts great power only to those who have proved themselves *faithful.*

## My Testimony About Faithfulness

When I was first filled with the Holy Spirit, I went to a Kenneth Hagin Campmeeting. In July, just weeks before the Campmeeting, I knew I had been called of God to preach, because God spoke to me.

It sounded audible to me, it was so powerful! I heard His voice! As God spoke to me, the Spirit realm parted, my eyes were opened, and I had a vision. God showed me my ministry, how He would use me, where He would take me, and so forth.

I was so overcome by this vision that all I could do was think about what I had seen! I just knew that one day I was going to step onto the platform of the world and the whole world was going to know who I was!

In my mind, I thought, "Oral Roberts, move over! Kenneth Hagin, make some room! Kathryn Kuhlman, your male counterpart has come!"

So I went to Kenneth Hagin's Campmeeting in Tulsa. There I sat, a young man full of dreams, visions, and aspirations about the work of the Lord. Oh, how I thank God for those early days! I never want to stop being a dreamer! But that week my imagination worked overtime!

I went to the services every night. I was waiting for that *grand moment* when Brother Hagin was going to step to the podium, pick up the microphone, and say very mystically, "Yes, yes, yes... Yes, Lord...this section over here? He's sitting over in that section? And uh...yes, yes, yes...uh, his name is Ri...Ric...Rick...Yes, that's right! His name is Rick! His last name? Re...Re...Ren... Uh, it sounds like Renn... Oh, yes, I see it, Lord. The last half of his name is the reverse of the first of his name. That would make his name Ren...ner. Hallelujah, I've got it! RICK RENNER! His name is RICK RENNER!"

I could just imagine hearing Brother Hagin say, "Is there a Rick Renner here tonight, sitting right over there in that section?" I imagined seeing myself *humbly* rise from my obscure seat and say, "Yes, Brother Hagin. Yes! It's me! *I'm Rick Renner!*"

In my young mind, just filled with the Holy Ghost, excited, with my *nothing-is-impossible attitude,* I could hear Brother Hagin say, "COME FORWARD! God has called you this night into a worldwide ministry! The Holy Ghost says to ordain you this night, set you in ministry, and let you preach your first sermon here tonight before these thousands!"

How sad! After attending all those meetings, night after night, it never happened. I was so disappointed! In retrospect, I am so happy it *didn't* happen! It would have been the quickest, worst sermon ever preached. I was not ready. How silly for me to have thought such things!

Silly as that sounds, many people are waiting for such a supernatural phenomenon to take place to catapult their ministry into worldwide acclaim. It doesn't happen this way! God uses men and women who are tested and proven "faithful."

## How I Learned Faithfulness

Just after this, I went to college. Instead of studying college material like I was supposed to, I majored in all the weird spiritual phenomena of the Charismatic Movement. And I was somehow involved in all of it. I *refused* to let anyone be more "spiritual" than I was!

Just weeks after joining a local church fellowship, I went to the elders to make sure they knew who I was: a giant man of God in their midst! I told them I'd be happy to help them out with their sermons anytime they needed help. I added I was available and, really, they *should* take advantage of my great anointing.

One week later, I was called to another elders' meeting. The leaders gathered around me and said, "Rick, it is true that you are anointed. In fact, we easily see the call of God upon your life. Therefore, God has told us to give you an important position in the church."

I thought, "Well, finally! It is about time that someone recognizes my great spirituality!" Then the elders continued, "We have heard from God, and we believe you should have a position. Starting this next Saturday morning, we want to give you a position in the Housekeeping Ministry. We want you to vacuum the carpets of the church building."

I was *appalled!* What — vacuum the carpets? Waste a great anointing on something as trivial and mundane as that? Yet, I did it. Week after week, every Saturday morning, I loaded up my car and headed for the church to vacuum.

To make matters worse, the church carpeting was a horrible pinkish-yellow color and it was covered with coffee stains! After scrubbing those stains and vacuuming all morning, it was hardly noticeable that I had done anything.

But I did it *faithfully.*

Then the elders called me in for another meeting. "Rick," they said, "we have seen your faithfulness in the Housekeeping Ministry, and God has spoken to us. It is promotion time for you." I sighed with relief, thinking that finally this degradation was over. Then they said, "We want you to stop vacuuming the carpeting and start setting up all the chairs for the service."

"WHAT!" I thought to myself. "Haven't I proved myself faithful yet?" But I did it. Week after week, every Saturday afternoon, I loaded up the car and headed for the building to set up the chairs.

Little did they know what they were asking for! I tried every chair arrangement possible! By golly, if I was going to do this, I was going to find a way to seat the most people possible. So one week, people would come to church and find the chairs set in a theatre-house style. The next week, we'd have church-in-the-round. The next week, the chairs would be arranged in a giant horseshoe. I was *trying* to be faithful to this job!

The elders called me again. This time they promoted me to be Door Greeter, then Songbook Hander-Outer, then Coffee Cup Washer for our coffee house ministry, and so on.

Finally, I was asked to teach during a Wednesday night meeting. By this time, I was so happy to be used by God that I didn't care if anyone recognized my deep "spirituality" or not. I was just thankful for the opportunity to be used! That night I taught for one hour and fifteen minutes! I was so happy to be used!

You see, it *didn't* matter that I thought I could teach better than they could. It *didn't* matter that I thought I had deeper revelation than they had. This was unimportant. *God was concerned about the condition of my heart and my faithfulness.*

Those early days, difficult as they were on my flesh, are the foundation for my obedience to God today. Because I learned faithfulness then and did what I did not want to do, it created within me a willingness to serve and obey.

My fierce determination to obey God *today* can be directly traced back to those early days. Because of that early obedience and faithfulness, today I obey God even when my flesh despises the task and finds obedience difficult.

*Faithfulness is the foundation for usefulness in God's kingdom:* "And I thank Christ Jesus our Lord, who hath enabled me, for that he counted me faithful, putting me into the ministry" (1 Timothy 1:12).

## A Proper Heart Attitude

Qualification is not enough! *Faithfulness is the issue.* That is why the Bible says, "commit yourself to *faithful men.*" Then Paul continues, "who shall *be able. . . .*"

The word "able" is extremely important to our study. In Greek, it is the word *hekanos* (he-ka-nos), which conveys the idea of "sufficiency." Notice how Paul speaks of the faithful men. He says, "who shall *be able. . . .*" Or, you could translate it, "who shall *be sufficient. . . .*"

Paul is teaching that "faithful men" may not be qualified for the task *right now,* but because of their proper heart attitude, they *can become* sufficient for the task. You see, God doesn't call people because of talent. God doesn't call people because He is impressed with their qualifications. *God calls you because your heart is right!*

## Ministry Doesn't Begin in the Pulpit!

I recently met a man who wanted to be used of the Lord. I asked him what he was waiting on. He said, "Well, I am a garbage collector." He was embarrassed by his occupation, and thought no garbage collector could ever go into the ministry.

Do you know why he thought this? Because that is a dirty job. It's not like being a bank president or a physician. He was embarrassed about his job and didn't think he could ever be used of the Lord in full-time service.

*Most ministry does not begin in the pulpit.* Do you want to be used by God? How did you think it was going to start? Did you think God was going to hand you the pulpit out of the clear blue one day and say, "There! PREACH!" You'd better pray it doesn't happen that way! You won't be ready!

Ministry doesn't begin on the platform, either. Ministry begins by setting up chairs or sweeping the floor. A man or woman is not promoted instantly. Instead, let him be in training and discipleship first. Watch his or her life. Work with him and slowly bring him, little by little, into more responsibility.

Faithfulness, faithfulness, faithfulness!

## Are You Foolish Enough?

In First Corinthians 1:27,28, the Word says, "But God hath chosen the *foolish* things of the world to confound the wise; and God hath chosen the *weak* things of the world to confound the things which are mighty; And *base* things of the world, and things which are despised, hath God chosen. . . ."

These verses say Jesus called the foolish, the weak, and the base. If this is true, and you belong to Jesus, you fall into one of these categories: You are either *foolish, weak, or base! That* is who God calls!

The word "foolish" is the Greek word *moraino,* and it is where we get the word "moron." The word "weak" is the Greek word *asthenia,* which nearly always describes someone so weak that he is failing of strength. (It is this word that we would use to describe someone in "a comatose condition.") The word "base" is the Greek word for "shameful" or "ugly."

This means you are either a moron, are comatose, or are ugly! If you are the Lord's, then you fall into one of these categories!

You see, none of us is really qualified to serve the Lord. God doesn't call us because of our natural gifts; He calls us because our heart is right. And if a person's heart is right and is *willing* to be taught, this "faithful man" can become more than he currently is! That is why Paul said, ". . . faithful men, *who shall be able. . . .*"

Again, this word "able" in Greek is the word *hekanos,* which conveys the idea of "sufficiency." Paul says, "Timothy, they may not be the cream of the crop in the world's eyes, but you work with them. Start where they are, and develop them. Faithful men *can become sufficient* for the task! They are not able to do the job now, but *they will be able soon!*"

You can pick the most unqualified person around, and if he is faithful, he will soon be qualified! He or she may be a garbage collector right now, but if he is faithful, in time this person will be *transformed!* He or she may even be a fivefold gift in the raw!

What a miracle and joy it is to see someone raised up *through faithfulness* into a public position where he is now teaching God's Word.

## What Does This Have To Do With the Combat Zone?

If you've ever picked the *wrong* person to be in leadership, you know exactly what this has to do with the combat zone! Picking the wrong person to be your close associate can almost be *fatal!* This is how church splits start, financial disagreements begin, doctrinal differences come in, and so forth.

If you've been badly "burned" by a friend, or perhaps misused or abused by a friend, you know the hurt this causes. This doesn't mean we should put up a wall and stop making friends. Of course, we need friends! We are fellow believers! But the Bible says to look for "faithful" people who have *proved* themselves genuine and have shown themselves truly committed.

Then you must obey Paul's command: *Get back out there and develop close relationships again!* You must become *para* with these new people. Get alongside them, stick close to their side, for the sake of relationship and discipleship. They need more than your words; they need *your example.*

*If you've been hurt in the combat zone in times past, the only way you'll ever obey this command is if you open your heart to God, beckon His assistance, and "lay hold of a steady current of God's power which comes to you as a result of God's grace," as we saw earlier.*

In Second Timothy 2:3, Paul says, "Thou therefore endure hardness, as a good soldier of Jesus Christ." In the next chapter, we will look at the *necessary* preparation and mental attitude you *must* have to successfully live and *win* in the combat zone!

# Chapter 4
# Learning To Endure

In Second Timothy, Timothy was facing a *horrible* predicament in the Christian world: Thousands of his brothers and sisters in the Lord were being slain by a man on the throne by the name of Nero.

Their "combat zone" was *real* — it was actually causing early, premature *death* by means of *torture.*

Satan was infuriated that Jesus had been raised from the dead! With all of his fury, he released the power of hell to come against the Church!

*Even children* who professed to know Christ were being killed for their faith. Yet, the gates of hell did *not* prevail against the Church!

We have a letter written by a Roman governor to Emperor Trajan which says:

> **I do not know just what to do with the Christians, for I have never been present at one of their trials. Shall I punish *boys* and *girls* as severely as grownups? Is just being a Christian enough to punish, or must something bad *actually* be done? If the accused says he is not a Christian, shall I let him go? What I have done, *in the case of those who admitted they were Christians, was to order them sent to Rome, if citizens; if not, to have them killed.*** I was sure they deserved to be punished because they were so ***stubborn. I gave them three chances to save themselves by putting***

> ***incense on your altar*** **[speaking to the emperor]** ***and cursing Christ.***

In his letter, this governor mentions what he has heard about Christians. He writes:

> **I have heard that a real Christian will not do this [renounce Christ or offer incense]. The Christians claim that they do nothing worse than meeting before dawn on a certain day and sing hymns to their Christ. They promise not to *steal* or *lie.* They also meet for a common meal [this was the Lord's Supper or Communion], though they have given it up since my order against *secret meetings.* I have had some women called deaconesses *tortured,* but could not find out anything worse than some crazy teachings and ideas. *Many* people had previously been touched by this foolishness and the *temples were nearly empty.* But now [since the persecution became so intense!] *the people are coming back to the temples again.***

The most famous example of Christian martyrdom is undoubtedly that of an 86-year-old brother in the Lord, Polycarp, Bishop of Smyrna. His martyrdom occurred 150 years after the death and resurrection of Jesus, and indicates that the fervor against Christians was *increasing* with time.

The story says that during a huge gathering of pagans, the mob began screaming, *"Away with the atheists!"* (This is what they called the Christians, because the Christians refused to burn incense to pagan gods.)

Suddenly in the midst of this growing riot, someone yelled, *"Get Polycarp!"* Polycarp, unafraid of death, wanted to surrender, but other believers persuaded him at first to hide in the country.

After Polycarp was discovered, a government official who was related to another Christian looked into the old man's eyes and asked Polycarp, *"What is the harm in saying,*

*'Caesar is Lord,' and putting incense on his altar and saving yourself?"* Polycarp adamantly refused.

Then the governor gave Polycarp three chances to save himself from being thrown to the lions in the great arena. After Polycarp refused the first two chances, the governor spoke to him again and said, *"Renounce Christ!"*

Polycarp answered, *"Eighty and six years have I served Him, and He has done me no wrong, and can I revile my King that saved me?"*

The governor insisted again, *"Swear by Caesar! I'll throw you to the beasts if you do not!"* The old bishop answered, *"Bring on the beasts!"*

The governor quickly replied with indignation, *"If you scorn the beasts, I'll have you burned!"* Polycarp looked him straight in the eyes and said, *"You try to frighten me with the fire that burns for an hour and you forget the fire of hell that never goes out."*

Infuriated by Polycarp's boldness, the governor yelled to the crowd, *"Polycarp admits he is a Christian!"* The crowd went wild, hollering and shouting. They said, *"This is the teacher of Asia, the father of Christians, the destroyer of our gods."*

The crowd then got huge bundles of wood and placed them around the feet of the faithful bishop. As the fire began to burn his flesh, tradition says that Polycarp prayed loudly:

> Lord God Almighty, Father of Jesus Christ, I bless Thee that Thou didst deem me worthy of this hour, that I shall take a part among the martyrs in the cup of Christ and to rise again with the power of the Holy Spirit. May I be an acceptable sacrifice. I praise Thee, I bless Thee, I glorify Thee through Jesus Christ.

## Padded Pews, Cushioned Chairs, and Pretty Windows

The early Christians had a real "combat zone" to deal with. They had no padded pews, cushioned chairs, stained-glass windows, steeples, Christian radio stations, television stations, and Bible bookstores. To be a Christian then literally meant a *life commitment*.

As difficult as it may be for us to imagine the persecution and martyrdom that was happening to our brothers and sisters in the Early Church, the real crisis was *not* their martyrdom. *The real crisis was the mass defections that took place!*

Did you notice what the governor's letter to Trajan said? "Many people *had* been touched by this foolishness and the temples *were* nearly *empty. But now the people are coming back to the temples again.*"

This crisis had revealed the *genuineness* of people's faith. Many forsook the Lord, deserted the faith, and went back to their old ways.

Timothy was seeing this take place in his own church, and was shocked to see it even among his *leaders*. They said, *"See you later, pastor! We're out of here until all the heat is off!"*

Timothy felt alone — isolated. All the men and women he thought were his friends had left, fearing they might lose their lives. They didn't want to be associated with Timothy or the church any longer. This was a very, very tough time for Christians.

Timothy definitely had a grudge to bear. And he had every *right* to have a grudge, be upset, and feel hurt. Every feeling he had was justified.

There are times when we do have a *right* to a grudge, but that grudge will do us no good. Grudges, anger, animosity, unforgiveness, and contempt do nothing but hurt our own life. That is why Second Timothy 2:1 is so important. Paul says, "Thou therefore, my son, be strong in the grace that is in Christ Jesus."

Timothy had a *reason* to be hurt. But he couldn't give place to that hurt, and *neither can you!* It is *too deadly*. That is why Paul's admonition to "lay hold of a steady current of God's power" is so vital.

Then Paul uses a word that modern people don't understand: COMMITMENT! He says, "the same *commit thou* to faithful men. . . ."

## Have You Ever Felt Betrayed?

Years ago, when I was one of the associates in a large Baptist church, I worked with many single adults. For one year I conducted a Divorce Recovery Program for those who were newly single. What an education this was for me and my wife!

That year I spoke to hundreds upon hundreds of newly divorced people. One after the next, they would sit across my big desk and tell me about their problems.

I would feel a tearing in my heart as they would share their crisis with me. Once they began opening their heart, there was no closing it. Like a gusher, tremendous hurt, pain, rejection, anger, confusion, and fear would come pouring out of them.

It was amazing to me, because they almost all told me the very same thing. One after another, women said, "How could he do this to me, when I was so faithful to him?" Or men would say, "I don't understand, Rick. I've been a good husband and a very faithful provider. How could she do this to me after all these years?"

Then, when I had finished listening and counseling with them, I would always invite them to come to the singles' Sunday School class to get to know other people.

Ninety-nine percent of the time they would say, "Oh, no! Nope, not me! I'm not going to stick my neck back out on the chopping block again! No, no, no — no! Why should I ever trust anyone ever again? After living all these years with my spouse, and he (or she) did this to me, what's my guarantee that it won't happen again? If I can't trust him (or her), I can't trust anyone."

Because of their hurt, which was *too great* to put into words, they were terrified that it might happen again. So they would hole up in their house, become a television addict, lose themselves in reading books, and so on. Why? They were afraid to trust again — even in a Sunday School environment.

It seems strange, remembering that. Why? Because now I hear *the same talk* coming from wounded pastors, church members, and devastated friends — people who have been wounded in the combat zone...

Yes, it's different people, but *the same talk.* "I can't believe he deceived me! After all that I've done for him! I put all of *me* into that brother!" Or, "It just kills me when I look at what has happened to our church. I'm so devastated, I don't know if I can *ever* go back again." Or perhaps, "Can you believe they did that to me? Isn't that the stupidest thing you've ever heard? I was so embarrassed. Are *all* Christians like *that?*"

Praise God, all Christians are *not* backbiters, deceivers, and liars. Some *are,* of course! But those few "bad apples" are so bad they tend to make us forget that there are piles upon piles of good apples in the basket, too!

## Here's Something You Must Remember

With all the scandals of recent years in leading ministries, moral failures, financial indiscretions, and crazy, ridiculous teaching that's been going on in the Church, it is very *easy* to become hard, skeptical, and sarcastic. *But we must not let this happen.*

Here is something to remember! When the Lord Jesus spoke to the seven churches of Asia Minor in Revelation chapters two and three, He was speaking to churches that had major problems. For instance, Ephesus had backslidden and lost its first love; Pergamos held to the doctrine of the Nicolaitanes; Thyatira had a woman named Jezebel who was seducing church members; Sardis was spiritually brain-dead; and Laodicea was lukewarm.

Do these sound like "trouble churches" to you? They had some very serious problems. You say, "All right, but what is it that you keep saying we *must* remember?"

Jesus called all of them *"golden"*! When explaining the vision to John in Revelation 1:20, Jesus said, ". . .the seven *golden candlesticks* which thou sawest are the *seven churches."*

Even with all their problems, Jesus still sees them as *"golden."* From man's perspective, they probably didn't look golden at all. Most of them looked spiritually bankrupt! Still, Jesus looked at them in all their mess and problems and called them "golden."

We must never forget that Jesus shed His blood for the Church. And even with all the problems of this hour in which we live, *He still loves His Church!* We must love it, too. If we do not, then we must *learn* to love it the same way Jesus loves it. It is His Body!

If you have been wounded by a part of the Church, then you must forgive them. If you cannot, then you must *learn* to forgive them.

At times I become angered at the foolishness that occurs in Spirit-filled circles. When I see a lack of good teaching, no evangelism, selfishness, false spirituality, frauds in the pulpit, lack of holiness, poor church commitment, and low tithing, it makes me wonder if my old denomination, the Southern Baptist Convention, may really be on the ball *better* than we are!

Jesus said in Acts 1:8, "But ye shall receive power, after that the Holy Ghost is come upon you: and ye shall be witnesses unto me. . . ." When I look at "Faith people," "Word people," or "Charismatics," I see very little witnessing — yet they are the ones who do all the talking about the Spirit's power!

At times I become disgusted with all of us, *including myself.* I feel there is a lot more *talk* than there is *action.*

That is when I have to remind myself: JESUS STILL LOVES THE CHURCH! With the obvious problems we have,

Jesus still looks at the modern Church, blemishes and all, and calls it *"golden"*! We are still "golden," saints! We must never forget this.

## Prescription for Wounded Warriors

However, many people who are a part of this "golden" Church are like a person who has wounded himself by ramming his arm through a plate glass window.

If, by accident, you put your arm through a large, glass window, it would hurt, wouldn't it? In fact, you'd probably rush to the emergency room to see if any tendons were cut, if major blood vessels had been severed, and to have your arm stitched back up again.

Let me ask you: Just because your arm is stitched up, does that mean your arm is immediately ready to be used again? No! Of course not. If you're not careful, you'll rip those stitches loose, and you may find yourself back in the emergency room having your wound stitched up again.

If you have been wounded in a relationship, it is very much the same. Dear friends, like physicians, surround you to check you out, make sure your heart is all right, and then sew you up. To get back out in the middle of the fight and place yourself in immediate jeopardy before your arm was healed would be foolish. You need healing. And that's *all right*.

But it's *not* all right to take advantage of the situation. Some have avoided church for years because of something that occurred 30 years earlier. They have held onto their hurts, grudges, resentments, and unforgiveness.

They've told their "horror story" a thousand times, hanging their wounds out for all to see, like evidence — a reason for "why" they should never get involved again.

*Are you going to let Satan do that to you?*

You must get things straight: We are living in a combat zone, and sometimes we get wounded; hit by a surprise attack. You're right — it's not fun. But we must recognize this is a possibility. Sometimes it just happens! Even good soldiers are taken by surprise.

While we should equip ourselves through prayer, study, meditation, praying in tongues, using our faith, attending church, and so forth, it is important for us to have made a *previous decision* that, if hit, we will be repaired, healed, and get right back out on those front lines again. *That is where we are called — to the combat zone!*

That is why Paul said, "Thou therefore, my son, be strong. . . ." Again, it is the Greek word *endunameo,* which speaks of an inner-strengthening or empowering; a deposit of power into the inner man. *God's power will hasten your healing process.*

There is no need for you to sit around "hurt" for weeks, months, or years to come. God's power is available to take care of the problem. With that kind of current flowing through you, it won't take long until you are ready to go for it once again!

However, "going for it once again" might be kind of scary to you. Those terrible wounds might still be very fresh in your mind. That's all right; it was uncomfortable for Timothy, too. That's why, in Second Timothy 2:3, Paul says, "Thou therefore endure hardness, as a good soldier of Jesus Christ."

## Enduring Hardness As a Good Soldier

When Paul says, "Thou therefore endure hardness, as a good soldier of Jesus Christ," he uses four Greek words which convey a very strong message to Timothy and to us.

Particularly notice the phrase "endure hardness," the word "good," the word "soldier," and the little word "of." These are all extremely important.

First of all, Paul says, "Thou therefore endure *hardness*. . . ." What does that mean? "Hardness" — what's that?

Because we are North Americans, we have not had to deal with much "hardness." Especially if you are younger, you missed all past wars; you never had to fight for the nation; you don't know what war does.

We live in a nation that is blessed. For the most part, we live in beautiful homes or nice apartments, and drive fairly new cars. And if we don't, at least they are accessible if we really desire them enough to work for them. We are called "the most blessed nation on earth," and we are!

Because of our blessings and protection from foreign aggressors, we have not had to deal much with "hardness." Oh, we may have to work overtime — and to us that is "hard." We may not get four weeks of vacation anymore, just three, and that can seem "hard." We may have to live in a house that has had the same carpet for six years, and that is definitely an inconvenience; we think it is "hard."

We might have to drive a car that is four years old, rather than a brand new one every two years, and that can be "hard," too. Sometimes we must mow our own yard, and that is very "hard." Right? Haven't you experienced some of this "hardness" in your own life?

Think about the society we live in. We have little or no knowledge about *real hardship* in our culture. And if someone preaches on "enduring hardness," we don't like that preacher too much, and we immediately start looking for another church!

This is one reason the Church of Jesus Christ is producing so little power in this hour! "Hardness" to most of us is "commitment."

We simply don't understand the phrase "enduring hardness." Don't misunderstand me; I'm like you! I like the blessings we possess in our great nation, and I thank God for them every day!

However, our "easy come, easy go" lifestyle has affected our spiritual commitment. If things get tough, rather than endure it and stay where God called us and fight it out, we say, "Well, if it's *hard,* it must not be God! If it was God, it would all just fit together nicely with no problems! You know, when God does something, it just falls together!"

Try telling that to the Christians of the first, second, and third centuries. Try telling that to Christians who right now — *today* — are living persecuted lives in other areas of the world. They know the real meaning of a "life commitment."

In no way, shape, or form is Rick Renner on a "suffering trip." No, I've been down that road earlier in my spiritual journey! This is not an invitation to suffer; it is a recognition of our need *to become tougher!*

Satan hates the Church, hates the local church as well, and wants to keep it torn up, divided, messed up, confused, and full of people who run away when things get "hard."

Had the believers of those early centuries taken this approach, the Church of Jesus Christ wouldn't have gone very far! *They were more committed to their task than their oppressors were to theirs!* The Christians knew what their mission was in the world. *They defied Satan and ten Roman emperors* who had them slaughtered with the most vicious deaths — *and they outlasted them all!*

We had better thank God that these early Christians were not "wimpy" in their Christian commitment. Oh, would to God that we were this committed today!

I can't imagine how large the mass defection would be if we in North America were subjected to the same persecution these early Christians experienced!

You see, to us, Christianity is getting together once a week to sing precious little songs, raise our hands, get "spiritual goose bumps," pacify our souls with soulish tunes, politely hold hands with our neighbor during prayer, give our weekly or monthly offering to the Lord, listen to a nice, non-threatening sermon, shake hands with the pastor, and wave at everybody as we drive off to eat our Sunday afternoon lunch with family or friends.

Ah, what a wonderful, *uneventful* life! No real challenge. No deep commitment is required, and everyone is so *sweet*! We can enjoy God with *no personal cost* to us; without paying any price!

Is this true? Do you think this is an accurate description of us?

It is powerful when you find a church that is genuinely committed! Their songs are filled with *war*! Their sermons are loaded with *conviction, challenge, and a call to higher commitment!*

Every week you walk away *confronted*, knowing what God is *requiring* of you! The gifts of the Spirit say more than, "Yea, I love thee, my children. . ." Rather, when God speaks, His voice echoes loudly, *like the voice of a Commander!*

Sickness is healed; demons are dealt with like enemies; slothfulness is not permitted; weak, wimpy, "don't-make-it-too-hard" thinking is non-existent; *and the saints view themselves as being in "ranks" in God's army!* This is powerful!

*This was the thinking required to survive the combat zone of the first century.* To really make an impact upon our world, it is *still* the *required* thinking for Christian soldiers!

## Take Your Place in the Ranks

That is why Paul advised Timothy, "Thou therefore endure hardness, as a good soldier of Jesus Christ." To conquer the crisis he was facing, Timothy, of necessity, had to possess a *warfare mentality.*

Notice Paul says, "endure hardness. . . ." This phrase in Greek tells us something very important about doing the work of the Lord. If you are going through a difficult struggle as you obey God for your personal life, for healing, for your marriage, for your finances, or for your church, this also applies to you.

The phrase "endure hardness" is actually a Greek compound word — *sunkakopatheo* (sun-kako-pa-theo) — three different words compounded into one to make a very important statement. The three Greek words are *sun, kakos,* and *pathos.*

While the phrase "endure hardness" is all right, it really isn't adequate to convey all that the Greek word actually means. There is much, much more in this word than first meets the eye. Remember, this phrase is made up of three different words, which means that hidden in the phrase "endure hardness" are *three different ideas.* This compound Greek word was carefully selected by the Holy Spirit!

The first part of the word is the Greek word *sun.* This little word *sun* always connects you to someone else; it is a partnership word. The idea is, "two are better than one." There are many examples of this.

For example, in Second Corinthians 6:1, the Bible says, "We then, as *workers together with him. . . .*" The word *sun* is used in the phrase "workers together with him."

"Workers together with him" is derived from a another Greek compound word. It is the Greek word *sunergeo* (sun-er-geo) — the words *sun* and *ergeo* compounded together.

The word *sun,* which, as we saw, conveys the idea of "connection" or "partnership," is attached to the word *ergeo,* which is the Greek word for "a worker." Placed together, these two words become *sunergeo.* It describes two or more partners that are working together on the same job.

In other words, we are not working *for* the Lord *by ourselves;* we are "fellow-workers with Him," "co-workers with Him," "cooperating with Him in our work." This is not merely a figure of speech. It is *God with us, doing the same job, at the same time, working together, cooperating as partners.* This is exactly what Paul means when he says "workers together with him." This is a description of "partnership" with God.

Another wonderful example of the word *sun* is found in Romans 8:26. It says, "Likewise the Spirit also *helpeth* our infirmities. . . ." The word *sun* is used in this word "helpeth."

The word "helpeth" is the Greek word *sunantilambanetai* (sun-anti-lam-ba-ne-tai), which is a compound of the words *sun, anti,* and *lambano.*

Again, the word *sun* conveys the idea of "partnership" or "cooperation." The word *anti* means "against," and conveys the idea of hostility. The word *lambano* means "I take." When compounded together, this tells us something wonderful about the Holy Spirit's "help" in our lives.

Because the Holy Spirit knows we cannot help ourselves in difficult predicaments, He comes *to join with us (sun),* and becomes our needed *partner* for the moment. He hates the work of the enemy in our lives, and He is *against it (anti).* And His desire is *to reach out and take* that infirmity into His own power *(lambano),* and remove it.

So when Romans 8:26 says, "Likewise the Spirit also helpeth. . . ," it means, "Likewise the Spirit also *becomes our needed partner, comes against that infirmity, and reaches out to take hold of it. . . .*" Thank God for the partnership of the Holy Spirit!

But back to the phrase "endure hardness." The first part of the word is *sun,* used in the two examples above (2 Corinthians 6:1; Romans 8:26) to convey *the idea of partnership.*

What about the next part of this Greek word? The second part of this compound word is the Greek word *kakos* (ka-kos).

*Kakos* is a very familiar Greek word. Most often in scripture, it is used to convey the idea of "something wicked, foul, or evil." It is used from time to time to describe those who were severely demon-possessed. *Kakos is always something bad, foul, wicked, or vile.*

If all you had were these first two words, *sun* and *kakos,* they would mean, "become a partner with this vile, wicked, horrible, foul situation." However, Paul goes further and uses a third Greek word, *pathos* (pa-thos).

*Pathos* is another well-known Greek word. It normally describes suffering, but when you study it out, it has more to do with *mental suffering* than it does *physical suffering.* For instance, this is where we get the word for a "*path*ological liar," or someone who is a "psycho*path.*" *It indicates a suffering of the mind.*

You may say, "What? Suffering of the mind? What does all this have to do with being a good soldier of Jesus Christ?" This is a very important word for Christian combat fighters!

You see, this was a word that was perfectly suited for Timothy, who was suffering *socially* and *mentally* — and perhaps would suffer *physically* in the near future. So great was the stress and rejection he had endured that it began to affect him *mentally.* This is why Paul's words in Second Timothy 1:7 were so vital: "For God hath not given us the spirit of fear; but of power, and of love, and of *a sound mind.*"

*Timothy's mind was beginning to bend!* Have you ever been in such an intense situation that you thought your mind might break? Have you ever been pushed up against the wall so hard, with no way out, that you thought you might have *a nervous collapse?*

What if you knew the government had your name and planned to kill you after torturing you first — and they weren't going to tell you when they were going to arrest you and take you away? You would think and think and think about it, *probably until it began to affect your mind!*

To us, this may seem to be an unrealistic example, but it wasn't for Timothy. Nero was killing many of his friends with a vengeance! Timothy knew his number would be up soon, too! He probably wondered which method of death they would use on him. Would they burn him, stone him, hang him, crucify him, or fillet him with a knife?

He must have wondered what it *felt* like to die a martyr's death. Every time someone knocked on the door of his house, Timothy probably wondered if it was the Roman authorities, come to arrest him. It would be very normal to be overwhelmed, subdued, and mentally affected by such a situation.

This is why Paul said, "endure hardness," using the three words *sun, kakos,* and *pathos.* Compounded together they mean, "Join in as a partner with the rest of us *(sun)* who are soldiers for the Lord; face the vile, horrible, foul, ugly circumstance *(kakos)* that is all around you; and if you must, then suffer *(pathos)* to get the job done!"

There were several key messages to Timothy in this word. First, he was not the *only* soldier serving the Lord. While it *looked* like everyone else had abandoned the Lord, many were still faithful.

Therefore, Paul says, "Join in as partner with the rest of us." It is as though Paul says, "Boy, you're not in the mess *alone!* Your problems are not special! A bunch of us are facing the same dilemma right now! Rather than run away from it, join in with the rest of us combat zone soldiers."

Second, by using this word *kakos,* it is as though Paul says, "Yes, you're right! It's getting pretty bad out here in the combat zone! In fact, it's never been *worse.* Right now, this is a bad, foul, wicked situation we're facing." It was good for Timothy to hear he wasn't the *only* one facing trouble.

Third, Paul tells him to "suffer" if he must. This is not because Paul is on a suffering trip. Absolutely not! Paul knew what it was to suffer, and he didn't want to believe that on anyone! *However, a job needed to be done, and if it meant suffer to get the job done, then suffer, if you must.*

Every Christian soldier who is committed to taking ground for the Kingdom of God must have this mentality.

## Is It Fun To Suffer?

There are some people who think it is *fun* to suffer. These people need to see a psychiatrist. Suffering is *not* fun!

When I pastored my church years ago, we had a few people in our church who were on a suffering trip. Every time I saw them, they were either being "broken, crushed, emptied, or chastened by God." They *never* had any joy.

I would see them one month and ask, "What is God doing in your life?" They would answer, "Oh, pastor, God is *breaking* me. I don't know how much more of this I can take!"

The next time, the conversation would be very similar. I would ask, "Tell me, what is God doing in your life?" "Oh, pastor," they would say, "the last time you asked, God was breaking me. It's gone *beyond* that, and now God is *crushing* me!

"We are not able to pay our bills, our children are sick, and we have bad marriage problems. Somehow, through it all, God is trying to use these things to conform us *into the image of Jesus!*"

Do you know what this is? It's *stupidity!* God's primary objective in life is not to *break* us, but *to make us whole!* You see, the reason we came to Jesus was because we were already broken — broken by Satan's destruction in our lives.

Jesus didn't come to break us, but to make us! Besides, a real chastening of the Lord always produces *fruit,* not disaster! Hebrews 12:11 says, "Now no chastening for the present seemeth to be joyous, but grievous: nevertheless afterward it yieldeth the peaceable fruit of righteousness unto them which are exercised thereby." Fruit, not destruction!

## Too Poor To Purchase Diapers

When we lived in Arkansas years ago, I was on a suffering trip. I thought *poor* was *holy.*

If poor means holy, then we should have been the holiest people on planet earth! At the time, we had only one child, Paul, and he was a baby. At times we were so broke, we couldn't even afford to buy *diapers!*

I thought it was holy to rely on other people to meet our needs! Oh, we were serving the Lord, and we were *so* holy!

One day when I came home from the office, Denise asked, "Rick, did you eat potato chips at the office today?"

I said, "Yes, honey."

She asked, "Were they good?"

I answered, "What's the big deal about potato chips? Why are you interrogating me like this?"

She said, "Rick, I'm a nursing mother, and I haven't had anything to eat today. Can you please tell me, were the chips good? Can you go back to the office and bring them home?"

You see, we had *no groceries* in our house and *no money* to buy them.

*We had no refrigerator, either.* But that was all right, because we had *no heat* on the bottom floor of the house. It got so cold in the kitchen, we didn't really *need* a refrigerator.

If someone brought us milk or frozen food, we'd just put it in the kitchen cabinets. The next day we wouldn't be able to use the milk for hours, because it had frozen solid during the night.

The bathroom was right above the kitchen, and the kitchen had *no ceiling.* One day, Denise and I were standing in the kitchen, talking, when I noticed water was dripping from all the exposed electrical wires in the ceiling.

I dashed upstairs and discovered the plumbing in our 99-year-old bathroom was leaking. Because it was running down the electrical wires, we turned the electricity off, fearing a fire.

That night before we went to bed, I placed big buckets under those leaks to catch the water. Then Denise, myself, and the baby went upstairs to the one room of the house that had heat. We crawled into bed, snuggled up to stay warm, and went to sleep.

The next morning I heard our little dog shriek as though someone had slapped her. I jumped out of bed, ran down the back stairs, and found to my surprise that those buckets had overflowed. Water had spilled all over the floor, and because there was no heat in the kitchen, all the water had turned into ice. *Our entire kitchen floor was now a giant skating rink!*

The poor dog had come running into the room to get something to eat and slid clear across the room. Now the dog was sitting in the corner, too terrified to move!

We actually lived like this and thought it was God's will! So when I say I've been on a suffering trip, I really mean business! My family has been down that road once.

We thought, "Oh, we're suffering for Jesus! Somehow this is conforming us into the image of Jesus. This is a life of holiness."

That was *not* holiness; that was *poverty!*

## When You Must Face Your Greatest Fear

This is not the kind of "hardness" Paul is talking about. Paul is not saying, "Get cancer — oh, boy!" This is not the kind of suffering Paul is talking about.

When Paul says, "endure hardness," he means, "Timothy, you're not the only one who has been wounded on the battlefield. The rest of us have, too. Quit thinking you're the only one who's ever been through hardship and join in with the rest of us who are faithfully fighting it out — you must come to grips with the horrible situation around you.

"It doesn't look like it is going to change and, in fact, it might get worse before it gets better. Rather than live the remainder of your life in fear, rise to meet the occasion.

"*Face your fears* and, if necessary, suffer to get the job done. Suffering is no fun, but someone must do the job. And if you must suffer to get the job done, then suffer. Even if your mind is under great stress, keep doing your ministry anyway."

Today we would say, "Grow up and face the facts! Be a man! Quit hiding from reality! Deal with this emergency and calamity like the rest of us!"

*Everyone has different fears.* Your fear may be different from the next person's. In fact, you may feel your fear is "silly." But that doesn't change it. What you fear, someone else would never fear. And what someone else fears, perhaps you would never fear.

Fear is relative to each person's own situation. One fears defeat, another fears sickness, and another fears rejection. While these fears are not God's will, nevertheless, people carry residual fear from past experiences.

Whatever it is that you fear, whether it be sickness, failure, rejection, hurt, insecurity, trusting others, or something else, it will *not* change by your hiding from it. Shutting your eyes and pretending it isn't there won't help you, either. Thinking, "Maybe it will just go away" will not make it go away.

In order to conquer your fear, you must *face it.* As long as you fear it, it will still exercise authority over your life.

Like Timothy, you must lay hold of God's power, rise to meet the occasion, and overcome. God will help you do this. *He is for you!*

## What Is a Good Soldier of Jesus Christ?

Paul continues this warfare mentality in Second Timothy 2:3 by saying, ". . .endure hardness, as a *good* soldier. . . ." This brings us to the second important word in this verse, the word "good."

The word "good" in Greek is the word *kalos* (ka-los), which speaks of something that is "good, beautiful, fine, excellent, fit, capable, or virtuous." By using this word, Paul is not just describing a solider, but an "excellent soldier," or a "fine soldier," or a soldier who is "fit, capable, or beautiful."

This soldier possesses all the correct "virtues" that a Roman soldier should possess. This describes a "good" soldier. We will see the full training, requirements, and virtues of a Roman soldier in Chapter 6.

You must keep in mind, Paul was writing in a day when the Roman Empire had conquered the world. To use this symbolism was very significant. The "virtues" of Roman soldiers were well known. They were skilled, disciplined, committed, fierce, driven, and hard-working men.

Often in the New Testament, Paul uses *military* language to refer to himself, his friends, and the Church-at-large. By using this terminology, Paul tells Timothy what God *expects* from him, from us, and from every member of the Body of Christ.

If you desire to be a leader in the Body of Christ, you must know that this will make you different from others. While the lay person is involved in the battle, too, leaders are subject to attack *more frequently* than people who are simply a part of the congregation.

*Leadership and fivefold ministry gifts are under constant bombardment from Satan,* because Satan knows their important, strategic place in the Church.

Satan is working a diabolical plan to destroy every apostle, prophet, evangelist, pastor, and teacher he can reach. If he can hit one of these and knock them off, he can wound the entire Church with *one* blow! This is war! The Apostle Paul understood this! Therefore, he uses militaristic language to describe our spiritual life.

The New Testament Church had a very militaristic view of themselves! They believed they were to "take the world" until all the world was evangelized and *converted.* So sure was their view of this, they literally changed their world and they changed history for all time.

The Early Church didn't sit around and "wait" for another "wave" of the Spirit before they rose up in power! They had *already* received power; they knew what Jesus wanted them to do; and they *did* it. To get this mission accomplished, they sacrificed everything.

This is why Paul now uses military language, telling Timothy to be "a good soldier of Jesus Christ." He often referred to himself as a soldier; he referred to Timothy as a soldier; and he even referred to Jesus as a soldier.

He says, "a good soldier *of* Jesus Christ." The little world "of" can also be translated "like." So Paul means, "Be a good soldier *like* Jesus Christ." He calls Jesus a soldier!

You won't find an ooey-gooey, "goose bump" mentality in Paul. He was very militaristic and barbaric in his commitment to the Lord. He cut no slack for his flesh at all. He knew he had been called of God, and he was going to do *whatever it required* to finish the job God had called him to do.

## Salute the Saints!

This militaristic mentality was reflected in nearly all of Paul's relationships and epistles. For instance, in Romans 16:7, he greets the saints in Rome. Rather than saying, "Tell the guys in Rome 'Hi' for me," like we would, Paul says, "*Salute* Andronicus and Junia, my kinsmen, and my fellowprisoners. . . ."

Does this sound like "regular" church talk to you? When you enter the door of your church on Sunday, do you turn around and "salute" those inside the building? How many times have you called yourself "the prisoner of the Lord"? Do you hear that kind of talk when you go to church? This was *not* allegorical speech.

*Paul was saluting others who were fighting on the front lines of a real battle!* Many of them were truly imprisoned on account of their faith and bravery. Because they preached the Gospel of the Kingdom of God, they were imprisoned not just because of faith, but because of *the political connotations* that accompanied their beliefs.

The message of the Kingdom of God was highly controversial and political in nature. It *demanded* allegiance to a higher Power, a higher King, and another Kingdom. For *this,* the Early Christians truly were suffering warfare.

Paul, who was in prison, along with Andronicus and Junia, who were prisoners in another city, were suffering for the Gospel, like members of an army that had been captured and taken by hostile forces.

Listen! This was the language of the New Testament Church! This was *reality* for them! They never had the privilege of simply being "Church people." Neither did they view themselves simply as a congregation. *They believed they were the army of the Lord!*

## The Great Commission or Little Commission?

When Jesus gave the Early Church the Great Commission, they took it seriously. Jesus said, "Go ye therefore, and teach all nations, baptizing them in the name of the Father, and of the Son, and of the Holy Ghost: Teaching them to observe all things whatsoever I have commanded you. . ." (Mark 16:19,20).

Couple this with Acts 1:8 — "But ye shall receive power, after that the Holy Ghost is come upon you: and ye shall be witnesses unto me both in Jerusalem, and in all Judaea, and in Samaria, and unto the uttermost parts of the earth" — and you discover that this Early Church really believed they were to take the entire earth for Jesus Christ; *not* just *affect* it. They were committed to *take* it!

When I was growing up, like most other Christians, I thought this verse meant, "*Try* to go into all the world. *If you can,* send missionaries to *some parts* of the world to try to win *some* in every nation. You'll never win them all, but try to win *some.* Although it's really not possible, *try* to win *some* in every nation. Of course, it will *never* happen, *but give it your best shot* to bring the Good News to every segment of society."

Do you know what we've done? We've taken the "Great Commission" and turned it into the "Little Commission"! Our thinking says, "Go into every nation and try to win *some,* if possible." What's "great" about that kind of a commission? This is not what Jesus intended!

The intention of Jesus was not for us to just "reach a few" in every country, or to send missionaries to "just a few" places in every country. The intention of Jesus was that we, His Church, would rise up *so strong* in the Spirit, and so *militant* in our faith, that we could literally *reach the entire world* and make *every member* of *every nation* a disciple of the Lord Jesus Christ!

The Early Church believed in a *worldwide conversion* and were giving their lives to see it happen! They knew the "whole world" needed Jesus Christ!

## That Is a "Great Commission"

The parallel verse for Acts 1:8 is Psalm 2:8, which says, "Ask of me, and I shall give thee the heathen for thine inheritance, and the uttermost parts of the earth for thy possession." The Early Church was asking for *that!* They wanted the *world!*

This is why their message had such political overtones. They were AN ARMY ADVANCING TO TAKE THE WORLD FOR JESUS CHRIST!

The New Testament Church had *this* kind of mentality! They were committed. . .they were going to take the world. . .they were going to conquer. . .they were going to turn the world upside down. . .and they gave their lives for this cause. . .they defied Satan. . .outlasted ten demon-possessed Roman emperors. . .and *did*, in fact, change the world!

Some were thrown in jail; some were killed; some were imprisoned. They viewed themselves as a militant Church! Yet, the weapons of their warfare were "not carnal" (2 Corinthians 10:4). Their weapons worked "By pureness, by knowledge, by longsuffering, by kindness, by the Holy Ghost, by love unfeigned, By the word of truth, by the power of God, by the armour of righteousness on the right hand and on the left" (2 Corinthians 6:6,7).

With this Spirit-given armor, they were driving back the forces of hell! Therefore, it was logical for them to use *military language* when they spoke to one another. This is why Paul said, "*Salute* Andronicus and Junia. . . ."

In Romans 16:9-16, Paul salutes many fellow-warriors. He says:

"*Salute* Urbane. . . ."

"*Salute* Apelles. . . ."

"*Salute* Herodion. . . ."

"*Salute* Tryphena and Tryphosa. . . ."

"*Salute* Rufus. . . ."

"*Salute* Asyncritus. . . ."

"*Salute* Philologus. . . ."

"*Salute* one another. . . ."

"*Salute. . . salute. . . salute!*"

It is almost as though Paul says, "Tell my comrades hello for me. I *salute* them! *Salute! Salute! Salute!*" Imagine how powerful the Church would be today if we had this same type of thinking! This is still God's plan for the Church today.

## Where Are the Front Lines?

Do you see how Paul's mind thought militaristically? *He lived in the combat zone!* That is why he tells Timothy to be "a good soldier of Jesus Christ." Do you know where Timothy was fighting? *On the front lines!*

You say, "Where are the front lines of battle today?" THE LOCAL CHURCH. Thank God for Bible school! While you may go through some real spiritual fights in Bible school, that is not really the battle field.

When you get into the local church and put all your knowledge to work, *that* is when the battle *really* begins!

When you get in your local church, *that* is when the devil *really* starts throwing darts at you from everywhere!

It is easy to read a book on healing, or to listen to a tape on prosperity. The battle begins when you begin *obeying* the Word. That is when the enemy comes to attack. This may be your battle ground.

You will have every opportunity to pack your bags and split the scene. There will be times when you will want to look for greener grass elsewhere. It always looks *so* good on the other side of the fence — *until* you get there! Then you find out it is the very same over there.

God has called you and me to fight *right where we are.* We are to take the land *where we are.* And if it gets tough *where we are,* then this is our opportunity to join with other brave men and women fighters, face the reality of opposition, overcome it, and get the job done — *even* if it causes our lives to be temporarily uncomfortable.

You *are* to be tough! You *are* to endure! You *are* to face anything! You *must* join in with the other soldiers until the battle is over and won!

This is why Paul says, "Endure hardness — join with the others who are fighting, face the vile circumstances, and if it means suffer, then suffer, but do whatever it takes to get the job done."

This is extremely important for us to understand if we are going to live and fight in the combat zone! It will *require* this kind of thinking on our part.

Back when I pastored, a man came to me and said, "Rick, God has told us your church is where we are supposed to be committed." He continued, "The move of God we have been praying for is going to start right here." He concluded, "We are here until Jesus comes again. *You can count on us!"*

My heart jumped a beat! I was *so* excited. Our church was new, and these people were an answer to our prayers. "Praise God," I thought. "Here's someone who will stay with us, help us, tithe, work, and try to reach the city with us!" They were exactly what we had prayed for!

Do you know how long they stayed? *Three months.* To my dismay, they were the type of people who went from one church to another, offering pastors false hope and empty promises.

Do you know why they left? Because they had given it three months, and the "great move of the Spirit" hadn't occurred yet. They left our church and repeated their empty promises to the next pastor whose church they attended.

"Pastor," they said, "we have come to your church from Rick Renner's church. We thought his church was the place to be, but now we know that *this* is the place to be. *We are here with you until we see this move of the Spirit begin.*"

When the revival didn't come after about three months, they left and went somewhere else. Can you see why a real revival doesn't come to most places? It is because God can't pin people down long enough to give them a revival! If God's people would settle down, revival would come!

## A Verse Spirit-Filled People Need To Know

A verse all Spirit-filled people need to know is Proverbs 28:19, which says, "He that works his ground will have abundant food; but the man who chases after fantasies shall have his fill of poverty" *(New International Version).*

Do you see what it says? "He that works his ground will have abundant food; but the man who chases [runs here and there, never sticks to anything, any job, anyplace, or any church] after fantasies [strange ideas, daydreams of a new wave of the Spirit, or a mystical, floating membership in the Universal Church only] shall have his fill of poverty."

There is a principle in this verse that we need to hear and apply to our lives. *If you stay right where you are, and if you work the ground where you are, you are going to produce a crop eventually.* It might take time, but you will produce a crop.

If you are chasing every little whim and notion that comes along all the time, you won't produce anything of real value for the Kingdom of God. You will *waste* your life chasing after dreams and fantasies.

We're all hungry and ready for a new, supernatural move of the Spirit. However, running here and there isn't a picture of stability! Ephesians 4:14 says, "That we henceforth be no more children [a picture of *immaturity*], tossed to and fro, and carried about with every wind of doctrine. . . ."

We must get in the army of God, fight the battle where we are, and "work our ground." Then we will have "abundant food." Then the supernatural move of the Spirit that we desire will take place.

## Preachers Do the Same Thing You Do!

I know a minister who constantly chases after fantasies. At one time, I did this habitually in my own life. What a shame!

This minister had a beautiful anointing on his life, but it produced absolutely nothing, *because* he wouldn't stay in one spot long enough to do anything for God!

He said, "God has called me to be a traveling evangelist. He wants me to evangelize the eastern portion of the United States."

So he gave it *six months*. After six months, his finances were still suffering badly, and he said, "I'm called to be a missionary to Australia."

"Wait a minute," I thought to myself. "Can't God make up His mind? First he said God called him to be an evangelist, then a pastor, and now a missionary to Australia. If he's hearing God, God doesn't sound very stable to me!"

This man needed to understand the principle of Proverbs 28:19: "He that works his ground will have abundant food; but he that chases after fantasies will have his fill of poverty" (NIV).

The truth is, when God calls you to do something, and it is hard, your mind tends to *drift* to other things. If you aren't truly committed to what God told you to do — right where you are — you will be tempted to think your drifting mind is the leading of the Spirit. Do you understand what I'm discussing here? Have you ever experienced this "drifting" feeling?

*Nothing* that changes this lost world and drives back Satan's forces is easy! What God has called my wife and me to do in our ministry is not easy, either. Our ministry has grown so fast, sometimes I am nearly overwhelmed by it. As God blesses this ministry, the responsibility grows greater and greater.

If I allowed my mind to drift, it would. It would drift to Montana, Wyoming, or perhaps Colorado. . .to some other place where life would be easier and the landscape would be beautiful. Oh, tall mountains, sweet-smelling pines, and fresh snow. . .

But that is not God's will, and I could *never* fulfill His plan for my life if I followed these "drifting" notions.

## Just When Your Breakthrough Is About To Occur

This type of thinking usually comes when you are on the brink of an incredible breakthrough. Usually, God is just getting ready to break through and hell's forces are being driven back, but the pressure becomes too intense, you give in to fear, and you slip away to try your "luck" elsewhere.

It is difficult to "endure hardness." It can be *very* hard! Don't let anyone kid you: The devil hates what you are attempting to do in your city, your ministry, your business, or your family. He can't bear the thought of God winning *another* fight!

That is why you must "endure hardness." All God needs is *one* person who will endure hardness, stay right where he is, and fight until Satan is conquered.

*God is looking for combat zone fighters!*

This is why Paul's words to Timothy were so pivotal for Timothy's life. Timothy was scared. He was hurt. He was afraid he might be murdered! Timothy understood Paul's words mean:

If it means murder, *then face murder...*

If it means martyrdom, *then face martyrdom...*

If it means face vile situations, *then face them...*

If it means suffer, *then suffer...*

If God has called you to pastor, *then pastor...*

If God has called you to travel and teach, *then travel...*

If God has called you to evangelize, *then evangelize...*

If God has called you to prophesy, *then prophesy...*

If God has called you to apostolic work, *then do it...*

If God has called you, *then get the job done!*

You may ask, "Rick, doesn't this demand a great deal of us?"

Yes, it does. *It will require your life!* Are you going to follow Jesus and give your life as "a good soldier of Jesus Christ?"

## Chapter 5
# New Testament Soldiers Who Endured

Everyone has had to "endure hardness" at some point in life. Paul describes in great detail some of the "hardness" he endured in Asia. In Second Corinthians 1:8,9 he says:

> **For we would not, brethren, have you ignorant of our trouble which came to us in Asia, that we were pressed out of measure, above strength, insomuch that we despaired even of life.**
>
> **But we had the sentence of death in ourselves, that we should not trust in ourselves, but in God which raised the dead.**

Notice the first part of the verse, where Paul says, "we would not, brethren, have you ignorant of our *trouble* which came unto us in Asia. . . ."

The word "trouble" is the Greek word *thlipsis* (thlip-sis). This word *thlipsis* was used in a very old sense to convey the idea of a "heavy-pressure situation." In fact, one translator says it was first used to describe torture; *tying a man up with rope, laying him on his back, and then placing a huge boulder on top of him.*

This, indeed, would create *a very heavy situation* for the man underneath the boulder! He would be in a "tight place," "under a heavy burden," or "in a great squeeze."

By using this word, Paul means, "We were under a heavy load! We were under an unbelievably heavy amount of stress and pressure. We were in very tight circumstances. Our minds were being 'squeezed.' The life was being pushed right out of us."

At first you might think this referred to *physical suffering.* Of course, physical suffering is difficult, but the greatest suffering always occurs in the mind — *mental suffering.* You can have pain in your body, but it is *nothing* like pain in your mind.

In fact, you can have pain in your body and live with it, if your mind is still in control. However, when the suffering begins to work on the mind, the body will break and fold.

So Paul's greatest suffering in Asia was not physical, but *mental.* This is why he goes on to say, ". . .that we were pressed out of measure, above strength, insomuch that we despaired even of life. . . ."

Particularly pay heed to Paul's first statement, ". . .that we were *pressed out of measure.*" This is the Greek phrase *kath huperbole* (kath huper-bole) and is extremely important. It literally means "to throw something beyond." It also describes something that is "excessive and beyond the normal range that most experience."

By using this word, Paul says, "We were under an amount of pressure that is not normal. It was *far* beyond anything we had ever previously experienced. *It was excessive, unbelievable, unbearable, and far too much for any one human being to endure.*"

Then he continued, "above strength." This word "above" is important, too. It is the Greek word *huper* (hu-per), which always conveys the idea of "something excessive." In order to explain how bad his predicament really was, Paul keeps using words that sound like exaggeration.

It is almost as though he says, "Normal human strength would have never been sufficient for this situation. It was beyond that! It was far, far beyond human strength; this predicament required strength on a measure that I had never previously needed. *It was beyond me!*"

Then he says, "...insomuch that we *despaired* even of life...." The Greek word for "despaired" is the word *exaporeomai* (ex-a-po-reo-mai). It was used in a technical sense to describe "no way out." It's where we get the word "exasperated." This is a word used by individuals who were "trapped, caught, up-against-the-wall, pinned down, and utterly hopeless." We would say, "Well, sorry, buddy, but it looks like this is *the end of the road for you!*"

Then Paul continues in verse 9, "But we had the *sentence* of death in ourselves...." The word "sentence" in Greek is the word *apokrima* (apo-kri-ma), which in this sense speaks of "a final verdict."

Paul means, "It looked to us like the verdict was in, and we were not going to survive. The verdict was death for us and, in fact, that is what we were already experiencing in ourselves at that time. We felt the verdict of death already operating in our souls."

When all of these different phrases and words are looked at together, it becomes very plain that Paul's primary suffering at this moment was *mental,* not physical. He is describing mental agony on a measure few of us know about.

I would translate this passage like this:

> ***We would not, brethren, have you ignorant of the horribly tight, life-threatening squeeze that came to us in Asia. It was unbelievable! With all the things that we have been through, this was the worst of all — it felt like our lives were being crushed. It was so difficult that I didn't know what to do. No experience I've ever been through required so much of me; in fact, I didn't have enough strength to cope with it. Toward the end of this ordeal, I was so overwhelmed that I didn't think we'd ever get out! I felt suffocated, trapped, and pinned up against the***

> ***wall. I really thought it was the end of the road for us! As far as we were concerned, the verdict was in, and the verdict said "Death." But really, this was no great shock, because we already were feeling the effect of death and depression in our souls....***

What happened to cause so much mental stress in Paul's life? His friends forsook him! He faced death every day — and this is not a figure of speech! He *literally* faced the prospect of a grueling, horrible, persecuted death on a daily basis.

If every day you thought someone might show up at your front door and shoot you, fillet you with a knife, crucify you, beat you until you died, or burn you alive, it probably would begin to affect your mind a little, too. Yet, this was a daily threat Paul faced.

That is why Paul said, "We would not, brethren, have you *ignorant*...." You say, "Why did Paul want us to know about this? Was it so people would feel sorry for him?" Absolutely not!

Paul wanted us to know that everyone must endure hardness from time to time. *Even great spiritual leaders are confronted with devastating situations.*

With all his knowledge, revelation, and experience, Paul still *almost* broke mentally! That is not my idea about Paul; that is what Paul himself tells us in this verse. When the Word says, "we despaired even of life," it describes the most excruciating mental pressure!

Yet Paul *didn't* break, and he *didn't* die! If you hold on and fight right where you are, *neither will you!* Like Paul, you will win the victory and be able to say this happened that you should not trust in yourself, "...but in God which raiseth the dead: Who delivered us from so great a death, and doth deliver...." (vv. 9,10).

*God's delivering power is yours!* He will rescue you now, and He will rescue you again and again in the future. All He asks is that you stay there at your post; don't give in to pressure; don't let the devil win; and fight it out! If you remain faithful to your task, He will remain faithful, too.

## Slinging a Sledge Hammer for Jesus

After the death of Nero, an emperor more demon possessed than he came to the throne. His name was Domitian, and he was far worse than Nero.

*What Nero did to Christians looked like preschool entertainment compared to what Domitian did to Christians!*

By the time Domitian ascended the throne, Paul and Peter were already dead, and the other apostles had been martyred, too — except for one, the Apostle John.

Therefore, Domitian took great pleasure in seizing John, who was now in his eighties, and taking him to the whipping post. The devil wanted to make John's death a hideous one!

Tradition says they dipped John into a big vat of boiling oil, and it didn't kill him. In fact, it appeared that he was totally unaffected by the boiling oil! There was not even one burn or scratch on his body. Domitian was infuriated!

So they exiled John in the middle of the Mediterranean Sea on the small island of Patmos, ten miles long and six miles wide, which was noted for its rocky terrain, forbidding weather, and criminal element.

Patmos was the repository for murderers, robbers, and criminals of every kind. The criminals' punishment was to work at the bottom of mine shafts, deep in the earth, breaking up rocks.

After serving the Lord all those years, it appeared that John would finally meet death at the bottom of one of those mine shafts, slinging a huge sledge hammer — and he was an old man in his eighties whose only crime was that he served the Lord. The Romans' purpose was to work him to death; to kill him with a heart attack.

It you were in the same predicament, what would you do? Would you enjoy it? Would you be happy about it? John could have been very bitter. He could have prayed, "Jesus! *I'm ticked off!* I gave my entire life to You. I worked for You and served You! Is this what I get as my reward? Lord, thanks a whole lot! I should be home with my family, on Social Security, being pampered by my children, enjoying life. No! Instead, I'm here in the bottom of this stupid pit, slinging a giant hammer, getting my beard caught when I swing, working until I nearly fall down dead. Thanks a whole lot, Jesus!"

This could have been John's attitude. But it wasn't. John knew that this was his new opportunity to "endure hardness."

## The Lord's Reward for Those Who Endure

Notice how John describes himself in Revelation 1:9. He says, "I John, who also am your brother, and companion in tribulation, and in the kingdom and patience of Jesus Christ, was in the isle that is called Patmos, for the word of God, and for the testimony of Jesus Christ."

John's description of himself is very important. It reflects the mentality of *a great combat zone fighter!* He identifies himself by calling himself: (1) *a brother;* (2) *a companion in tribulation,* (3) *a companion in the kingdom,* and (4) *a companion in patience.* It is important that John used these four statement to identify himself. Let's see why.

In the first place, John writes, "I John, who also am your *brother. . . ."*

Why does John introduce himself as "a brother"? There is more here than first meets the eye. You say, "Well, he calls himself a brother because he is a Christian." Yes, that's true. But there is more to this statement than that.

By using this word "brother," John means to convey a message to others who are suffering like he is. He means to say, "Not only am I your brother in a spiritual respect, but I am your brother in affliction, in persecution, in problems, in struggles, in trials. . .you and I, we are the very same — we are brothers."

You say, "Rick, why is that so important?" Because everyone experiences hardships. At times you may think that great spiritual leaders escape hardships because their faith is so refined.

Yet, here was the great Apostle John on the Isle of Patmos, suffering as a criminal, breaking up rocks in the bottom of a mine shaft, working himself to the bone! John did not want sympathy, however. Instead, he wanted to encourage the saints! He wanted them to know that they were not alone in their predicament!

Something else here is important. Notice how John *didn't* introduce himself. He did not say, "I, John, the great, illustrious, powerful, anointed, special, well-known apostle of Jesus Christ. . ." He could have made those statements, but he didn't. Why didn't he?

When you are in the heat of battle — *living in the combat zone* — and a satanic attack is hitting you from every angle — some things cease to be important. Affluence, prestige, power, and notoriety are some of those things. It didn't really matter at this moment that John was *John,* the beloved disciple of Jesus.

When Satan's attacks are flying in your direction, and you are trying to dodge them as fast as you can while, at the same time, survive the occasional hits you receive, your popularity and celebrity status *cease* to matter. You forget all that!

All people, whether well-known or unknown, feel the same pain, the same hurt and, the same confusion, and experience the same struggles in the same manner you do. It is almost as though John says, "Let's forget who I am. Right now I am 'your brother.' "

Then John goes on to state the key ways in which he is experiencing brotherhood and unity with others. He begins by saying, "I John, who also am your brother and *companion in tribulation. . . .*"

The word "companion" is the Greek word *sugkoinonos* (pronounced sun-koi-no-nos), and conveys the idea of "sharing one common experience with someone else." It is a compound of two Greek words, *sun* and *koinonos.* The second part of the word, the word *koinonos,* speaks of "a common experience; something that everyone experiences, or something that is shared."

When the two words are combined into the word *sugkoinonos,* it describes "two or more persons who are joined together in partnership and are sharing the exact same experience together."

It is important that John uses this word. He is once again removing the stigma of "who" he is, and is saying, "I am your brother. In fact, you and I — we are partners together in this ordeal. What you are experiencing, I am experiencing, too. We are sharing a common experience. *We're in this together!*"

What John is experiencing through persecution, others are experiencing, too. At this time, this was the general situation that all believers were going through; they were all living and fighting in the combat zone.

But John doesn't stop there. He continues, "I John, who also am your brother and companion *in tribulation. . . .*"

This word "tribulation" in Greek is the word *thlipsis* (thlip-sis), the same word used by Paul to describe his difficult circumstances in Second Corinthians 1:8. Again, it conveys the idea of "a very heavy load, a burden that is crushing, or being pinned against the wall, pushed to the limit, forced to bear a load far too much for any individual to bear."

This was also good news for others who were suffering. You see, this was the testimony of all these early believers: They were forced to carry an excessively heavy burden. Life was difficult, hard to bear, and nearly crushing. John says to them, "I understand. I am your brother and fellow-partner in these crushing difficulties."

Why was it important for other believers to hear John was experiencing difficulties? Because he was a leader; the *only* remaining apostle first chosen by Jesus, and now a very old man. He was their primary example.

If John could endure at his advanced age, then they knew they could endure. If John was remaining true, then they knew they could remain true, too. They needed to hear victory in his words, and this is *exactly* what they were hearing through his writings to them.

John goes on to add something else very important: He says, "I John, who also am your brother and companion in tribulation, and in *the kingdom*. . . ."

You may ask, "Why is the mention of *'the kingdom'* so important?" Because this tells us John has never forgotten his most important identity. While the world viewed him as a political rebel and a maverick, and imprisoned him as a criminal, John was still very aware that he was a member of "royalty" — *a member of God's kingdom.*

It was for *this kingdom* and *the Gospel of the kingdom* that John was suffering. With all the persecution that had transpired, John has taken none of it personally. He knows the world is not really against him, but against the kingdom he represents.

Although he is now suffering for this kingdom, John knows kingdom rewards are his! And while he is indeed "a companion in tribulation," he knows that he must keep *a proper perspective* of things.

The real issue is not John; *the real issue is the kingdom.* John, and all his brothers and sisters, had to keep this in the forefront of their thinking. They had to be willing to pay *any price needed* to see this kingdom advance and take hold of a lost world. John was happy to be a soldier for the Kingdom of God, and he was proud to be a political prisoner on behalf of His King!

Then John mentions something else extremely important. He says, "I John, who also am your brother, and companion in tribulation, and in the kingdom and *patience* of Jesus Christ. . . ."

Especially notice the word "patience." This word is from the Greek word *hupomene* (hu-po-me-ne), and is a compound of two Greek words, *hupo* and *meno.*

The word *hupo* refers to "being underneath something." In this case, it is a picture of "being underneath something very heavy." The word *meno* literally means "I stay," and it describes "a decision to abide in one spot and not move away from it." Combined, these two words describe "the resolute decision of someone who is determined." He or she has decided "to stay at one spot forever, even if the load gets excessively heavy."

This word "patience" was the queen of all virtues for the First Century Church. Everyone aspired to this virtue. If a man or woman had *hupomeno* ("staying power" or "hang-in-there power"), he could endure any trial and last longer than any adversary. Therefore, all early believers aspired to have this virtue, and prayed to possess it. If you had it, you would *always* win!

By selecting this word, John makes his point clear: "Just like the rest of my brothers and sisters, I am under an unbelievably heavy load — a load so heavy it should crush me — but I have decided not to move! I know the Gospel is right. I know what Jesus Christ has done in my life. And I am not going to move!"

John's "patience" ("staying power," "hang-in-there-power") caused him to outlive his persecutor, Domitian! *Those who endure always win their battles in the combat zone!*

Then John explains "why" he is in Patmos. He says, "I . . .was in the isle that is called Patmos, for the word of God, and for the testimony of Jesus Christ" (v. 9).

It seems unfair to put an old man in the bottom of a mine shaft, work him nearly to the bone, and hope that he will die because of "the word of God, and for the testimony of Jesus Christ"! Really! This is not fair!

It *didn't* matter whether it was right or wrong. It was happening. What *was* important was for John to deal with it correctly, endure it like a good soldier, and come out the winner.

If you are going through a difficult time, the same applies to you. You may be tempted to think, "How did this happen? What did I do wrong? Why did God allow this to take place? How did I let Satan get in and do this to me?"

Your questions will *not* change your situation. What *is* important, is *that you deal with the devil's attack bravely, endure hardness IF YOU MUST, and come out of that combat zone the winner!*

Don't budge an inch! Don't give in to the devil's attacks! You stay in that spot God called you to; don't you dare move, even if the load becomes too much for you to bear! This "patience" or "endurance" will *put you over* and *put Satan under!* He has *no counterattack for patience!*

## How Would You Like This Reward?

In the midst of these trying circumstances, something wonderful happened to John: He received a special touch from God — *right in the middle of the combat zone* — to encourage him, keep him going, and let him know that the King and the kingdom he was suffering for knew of his plight.

John says, "I was in the Spirit on the Lord's day, and heard behind me a great voice, as of a trumpet, Saying, I am Alpha and Omega, the first and the last. . ." (Revelation 1:10,11).

John receives a personal visitation from the King! And what a visit this was!

Notice John says, "I was in the Spirit on the Lord's day. . . ." Two things are important to see in this testimony of John.

*First,* John says, "I was in the Spirit." *Second,* he mentions a specific day: "the Lord's day." Both of these phrases carry great weight and significance. Why? Because this tells us *how* this visitation took place; *what* John was probably thinking about when it took place; and *why* it took place on "the Lord's day."

First, John says, "I was in the Spirit. . . ." The word "was" is the Greek word *ginomai,* and this is very important. Why? Because the word *ginomai* indicates John did not know this experience was about to occur. This visitation with Jesus took him by surprise. He was not expecting it.

The word *ginomai* ("was") is almost always used to describe "something that develops slowly." Sometimes it is used to describe "something that occurs unexpectedly." For example, it is used in Acts 10:10 to describe how Peter's vision took place. It says, "And he became very hungry, and would have eaten: but while they made ready, *he fell into a trance.*"

The phrase "he fell into" is the Greek word *ginomai.* This is important, because it tells us Peter was not expecting to have a vision that afternoon. He was simply on top of the roof, praying and waiting for dinner, when — *ginomai!* — he slipped into a trance.

The idea of *ginomai,* as used here, indicates Peter *"fell into* a trance," *"slipped into* a trance," "somehow, having nothing to do with it himself, *came into* a trance," *"unexpectedly found himself* in a trance." The idea is that this took Peter by surprise.

John uses the same word to describe the events that happened to him in Patmos. He says, "I *was* in the Spirit. . . ." Again, the Greek word for "was" is the word *ginomai.* This indicates John means, "I don't know how it happened. . .I was not expecting this to occur. . .I looked up, and to my surprise, I had stepped out of this realm and over into the realm of the Spirit." This was unexpected and took John by surprise. This tells us *how* this visitation took place.

Moments earlier, John had been slinging a huge hammer in the bottom of a mine pit. But now, seconds later, he has been transported into the realm of the Spirit. He had not been praying for a special visitation, or wishing for an angel to appear. He was simply working hard in the mines when, suddenly, there — standing behind him — *the Lord Jesus Christ appeared!*

Next, *what* was John probably thinking about when this special visitation took place? The key is found in the phrase "the Lord's day."

This is *not* what it seems at first. It appears that John is talking about the Sabbath, or perhaps the first day of the week, Sunday, when believers gathered to worship the Lord. In both cases this is *wrong.*

What is "the Lord's day" mentioned here in this text? This is a definite reference to *paganism* and *emperor worship!* You may ask, "How do you know?" Because the phrase "the Lord's day" is from the Greek word *kuriakos* (ku-ri-a-kos), which was used in a technical sense to describe one day of the week set aside by the emperor, for the sake of emperor worship.

It was technically called "the Imperial Day," and was nearly always associated with this vile emperor worship. This was the day that all were commanded to worship and burn incense to the current emperor. What made it worse was, Domitian picked the Sabbath for his day of idolatrous worship, knowing this would offend Christians and Jews alike.

It was this vile, filthy, perverted Domitian who had exiled John to Patmos. As I noted earlier, in comparison with Domitian's persecution, Nero's persecution of the saints looked like preschool activity. Domitian was bent on killing Christians.

Not only this, but Domitian also had another demonic twist in his mind. In A.D. 83, Domitian had a coin minted, picturing his dead son. On the back of the coin, his dead son was pictured sitting on the globe of Earth with seven stars in his right hand — indicating heavenly dominion over the world.

Why is this important? Because it added another twist to Domitian's idolatry. He believed his dead son was working with him to conquer the world! Not only were you to worship Domitian, you were to worship his deceased son as well.

That is why Jesus appears in Revelation 1:16 with seven stars in His right hand. Speaking of Jesus, it says, "And he had in his right hand seven stars. . . ." This was symbolism John knew too well. He understood!

Jesus meant to convey, "I know that Domitian says his dead son is lord, but let it be known, *I Am the One who has heavenly authority over the earth, and no one else! I Am the One with seven stars in my right hand.* I Am Lord! Domitian and his dead son do not control you, John, or My Church. *I, and I alone, have heavenly authority. I Am Lord!"*

Now, however, John is working in the bottom of the isle called Patmos, working, working, and working, when suddenly he remembered what day of the week it was! He *probably* thought to himself as he slung that huge hammer, "Well, if my calculations are correct, this is the 'day' of the week Domitian demands everyone worship him — his 'Imperial Day.'

"I don't care what day Domitian says it is, or how many times he calls himself the lord, I will not worship this deranged, demon-possessed man. There is only ONE LORD — King Jesus! I'm not worshipping Domitian today. I'm going to worship JESUS CHRIST! Even though I'm in the bottom of this pit, and no one can see me, I'm going to worship with all my might!"

I can just hear John saying louder and louder and louder, "JESUS IS LORD! JESUS IS LORD! JESUS IS LORD OVER ALL!"

Suddenly, the veil of the Spirit parted, and John looked up to find himself no longer standing in that pit. As he says, "I was in the Spirit. . . ." That word "was" is again the word *ginomai.*

It is almost as though John says, "I don't know how it happened! All I know is, I refused to worship Domitian and I started to worship Jesus. I was swinging that hammer, breaking up rocks, when all of a sudden — out of the clear blue — I felt something happen!

"I dropped the hammer and realized *'I was in the Spirit.'* It was then, at that moment, to my surprise I heard a great voice, like a trumpet, behind me. . ."

This was a revelation of the Lord Jesus Christ that no one had ever seen before! People laugh at Oral Roberts because he said he saw a 900-foot Jesus. To be honest, I'm surprised Oral Roberts did not see a *10,000-foot Jesus!*

The Jesus that John saw on this day was not like the Jesus that John remembered: He had assumed a brand new appearance! What did Jesus look like? Why did this visitation take place on this abominable day of pagan idolatry and emperor worship?

The real King, Jesus Christ, was coming to see His great soldier, John. The King for whom John was "enduring hardness" had come to reveal Himself in all of His *majesty, power, and might!*

Jesus was dressed *in the clothing of an emperor* — with an imperial sash made of gold around His chest; kingly garments down to the foot; and His feet were as fine brass, as if they burned in a furnace.

John must have thought, *"O Jesus, You are my King!"* It didn't matter that all the civilized world was worshipping a demon-possessed man on that same day; Jesus was still Lord over all! And He was coming to reveal Himself to a soldier who had paid a very, very high price. Jesus was saying, "Yes, John, I Am the real Emperor!"

John says in Revelation 1:12-18:

> **And I turned to see the voice that spake with me. And being turned, I saw seven golden candlesticks;**
>
> **And in the midst of the seven candlesticks one like unto the Son of man, clothed with a garment down to the foot, and girt about the paps with a golden girdle.**
>
> **His head and his hairs were white like wool, as white as snow; and his eyes were as a flame of fire;**
>
> **And his feet like unto fine brass, as if they burned in a furnace; and his voice as the sound of many waters.**
>
> **And he had in his right hand seven stars: and out of his mouth went a sharp twoedged sword: and his countenance was as the sun shineth in his strength.**
>
> **And when I saw him, I fell at his feet as dead. And he laid his right hand upon me, saying unto me, Fear not; I am the first and the last:**
>
> **I am he that liveth, and was dead; and, behold, I am alive for evermore, Amen; and have the keys of hell and of death.**

*What a visitation!* Although John had paid a high price of persecution, and had to "endure hardness" in his situation, Jesus revealed Himself to John *in the midst* of John's excruciating circumstances.

Notice the words that Jesus, our Great Emperor and General, uses as He speaks to John in verse 18. He says, "I am he that liveth, and was dead; and, behold, I am alive for evermore."

Notice the first part of that statement: "I am he that liveth, and *was dead.*" The phrase "was dead" would be better understood, "I became temporarily dead. . . ." It describes for us how Jesus views His own experience of "enduring hardness" on the cross.

Although it was hellish in nature, it was but a brief "interruption" in His on-going, eternal existence. You could translate it, "I Am He that liveth, but once I became dead. . . ."

You say, "Why is it important to know that?"

Because Jesus is speaking to *a combat zone fighter* who is enduring much hardness. This must have been great encouragement to John's heart!

"Yes! Yes! Jesus, You, too, have been through hardness!"

But the Lord didn't stop there. He continued, ". . .and, behold, I am alive for evermore. . . ." Death was not able to stop Jesus Christ, and now the forces of hell and Domitian were not going to stop John, either! While John's situation was horrible, it was but a brief interruption. Soon, King Jesus was going to bring John out of this horrible pit and back to his Church family again!

## How the Lord Comes to Us

John was suffering as a soldier; therefore, he needed to hear from *his Emperor!* Jesus knew exactly how to come to John. He knew that John needed to know that the King and the kingdom for which he was "enduring hardness" were aware of his plight.

Perhaps your struggle is different. Maybe your problem is sickness. To you, Jesus Christ will reveal Himself as *the Great Physician.*

Is your problem mental afflictions? To you, Jesus Christ will reveal Himself as *the great Deliverer!*

Is your problem a church problem? To you, Jesus Christ will reveal Himself as the great *Head of the Church!*

Is your problem financial? To you, Jesus Christ will reveal Himself as *the great Provider!*

Those who endure temporary "hardness" not only will win the fight, but will also gain *a brand new perspective of Jesus Christ!*

As Paul continues speaking to Timothy in Second Timothy 2:4, he says, "No man that warreth entangleth himself with the affairs of this life; that he may please him who hath chosen him to be a soldier." This is where we will begin in the next chapter.

## Chapter 6
# Warring in the Combat Zone

Paul has been speaking to Timothy in military terms. He has told Timothy to "endure hardness," and has called him a "soldier of Jesus Christ" (2 Timothy 2:3). This militaristic mindset of Paul is used throughout all his epistles. He was serious about fighting and winning the war in the combat zone.

In Second Timothy 2:4, Paul continues using militaristic terminology. He says, "No man that warreth entangleth himself with the affairs of this life; that he may please him who hath chosen him to be a soldier."

In this verse, Paul employs five very significant words: "warreth," "entangleth," "affairs," "please," and the phrase "who hath chosen him to be a soldier." There is no question as to the implications of these words. Paul is clearly likening our spiritual commitment to that of Roman soldiers — and the best of Roman soldiers at that!

First, let's look at the word "warreth." The word "warreth" in Greek is the word *strateuomenos* (stra-teu-o-me-nos), from the word *strateuomai* (stra-teu-o-mai), which is the technical title for "a soldier."

The earlier form *(strateuomenos)* used here where Paul says, "no man that warreth. . . ." does not, however, describe a soldier's technical title but, rather, his *function*. What is his function? *To be in the habit of warring, fighting, killing, and conquering.* However, it also refers to the constant drill, military exercises, hardships, and training which were required of every Roman soldier.

*The average soldier was fully and regularly immersed in all the disciplines that accompany warfare.*

Once again you must keep in mind that this was a time when Rome had conquered the entire world with its great armies. To use such language in that day would definitely convey a special image to the reader. Immediately, *military scenes of men who were skilled, disciplined, hard, driven, mean, committed, and almost physically perfect, would come to mind.*

Everyone knew about the lifestyle of Roman soldiers: It was a constant, exercise-filled, rigorous lifestyle, intended to take a normal man and make him into a good man; to take a good man and make him into a great man; and to take a great man and make him into a perfect man. *They never stopped striving for perfection; they were committed!*

Because Paul uses this background to convey his message about commitment and warfare, we must take a look at history to see what it tells us about Roman soldiers.

## The Roman Soldier in New Testament Times

Here, in these words of history, we find the full backdrop to what Paul meant when he called Timothy a "good soldier of Jesus Christ." Veiled in history, we discover why Paul says to each of us, "No man that warreth entangleth himself in the affairs of this life; that he may please him who hath chosen him to be a soldier."

Flavius Vegetius Renatus, commonly called Vegetius (pronounced Ve-ga-tius), wrote the most influential military treatise ever known about the Roman soldier and army. He was a Roman of high rank. Although he lived nearly 300 years later (c. A.D. 380), he had the most extensive knowledge of the Roman armies and soldiers that has ever existed. No one had more superior knowledge about the Roman army of New Testament times than he.

Vegetius wrote a book about the earlier Roman armies which in time came to be viewed as a military "bible" for the later armies of Rome. *By the time Vegetius wrote, the armies had become lax, uncommitted, and unprepared for war.*

The great majority of soldiers themselves had become weak, physically fat, unexercised, and lazy, no longer viewing their right to serve as a *privilege,* but rather as a nasty, uncomfortable, unwanted *obligation.*

Unfortunately, this sounds very much like a description of the Church today! Because we've lived in a period of peace and prosperity, the army of God has become lax, and to a great degree — even with all its knowledge and teaching — the Church is unprepared for war. The great majority of the Church has become weak-willed, fat, unexercised, lazy, and no longer views the walk of faith as a privilege, but as a nasty, uncomfortable, unwanted obligation.

It was because of this military deterioration that Vegetius began to study the ancient ranks. The purpose of his exhaustive, in-depth study was to show *what an army in excellent condition should be like.*

It is from his early official records that we draw this information about the Roman army and the Roman soldier who lived during the days of Paul and Timothy. As you read this, you will notice the many applications to our own spiritual warfare and combat zone!

## The Perfect Soldier

Listen to how Vegetius describes the best recruits for the early Roman army:

> ***. . . the peasants are the most fit to carry arms* for they from their infancy have been *exposed to all kinds of weather* and have been brought up to *the hardest labor. They are able to endure the most intense heat of the sun,* are unacquainted with use of baths and are strangers to the luxuries of life. They are *simple, content with little, inured to***

> ***fatigue, and prepared in some measure for military life by their continual employment in farm work, in handling the spade, digging trenches and carrying burdens.***

Who does he say makes the best soldiers, and why? Peasants make the best soldiers, he says, because they are accustomed to extremes of weather, they are accustomed to hard work, they can endure heat, they are simple, they are content with little, they are immune to fatigue, and they are accustomed to such physical labor as digging and carrying burdens.

The question arises: "Why did these qualities make a man better suited for service? Why were these qualities so vital when it came to selecting the best soldiers?" Let us examine the six characteristics of the perfect Roman soldier.

First, warfare takes you through stormy, cold weather, rain, snow, sleet, and almost unbearable temperatures. *Regardless of the outward conditions, the war must go on.*

In the same way, when you begin fighting your "fight of faith," it is amazing how the weather of life can change on you without any prior warning! It seems like Satan knows just when to cause some bad events to blow into your life. He knows *exactly* when to attack you with some spine-chilling report. It seems one of his favorite tactics is to cause great changes in the climate right after you make a step of faith.

Does this change the *reality* of the fight? Are you going to allow Satan to scare you off to some other, more comfortable zone? When the sun disappears, the winds begin to blow, and the sleet begins to fall, what will you do? *You must keep fighting your fight of faith anyway!* Although it may look like the stormiest season of your life, the weather won't last long! If you are true to the fight, you will outlast the battle!

Second, Vegetius says that peasants are the most fit because "they have been brought up to the hardest labor."

Why is this important? Because combat with the adversary will involve the hardest work you've ever done! If you're afraid of hard work, you'll never get one thing done for the Kingdom of God.

*Combat zone fighters must be willing to do the hardest type of work!*

Third, Vegetius said that peasants "are able to endure the most intense heat of the sun." You'd better come to grips with this reality: It can get plenty "hot" when you're dealing a death-blow to the devil's strongholds! He'll fight you all the way to the end. *Soldiers in God's army had better be ready to "take the heat"!*

Fourth, Vegetius says, "they are simple." What does "simple" mean here? Does it mean stupid? Absolutely not. Simple means "uncomplicated." The best soldiers are simple — free from care — free from anxiety — free from worry — free from personal ambitions — free to do their job without any type of reservation.

To be a good soldier is their sole aspiration in life. This type of single-mindedness always marks the best soldiers; nothing gets in their way!

Fifth, he says they are "content with little." This doesn't mean we should embrace poverty; that isn't what he is saying. What, then, does he mean? Vegetius tells us that the best soldiers are people who don't *require* a great deal of comfort. That's why peasants were so good at warring: Life had never afforded much luxury to them; therefore, they weren't aware they were missing anything!

Often, when the blessings of God come into our lives, and our financial resources begin to grow, we forget where we came from. Adapting quickly to a new level of prosperity and blessing, we forget the fight of faith we waged in order to get there!

As good soldiers of Jesus Christ, we must never allow the blessings of God in our life to remove us from the combat zone and put us over into the comfort zone! *Even in peacetime, we must be willing to pay any price to win new territory for the Kingdom of God.*

Sixth, Vegetius says because peasants are "inured to fatigue," they always make good soldiers. What does this refer to? A willingness to keep working, fighting, and warring even when you feel like you've been pushed to the limit.

You see, peasants didn't have the privilege of saying, "I've done all I can do today, and I'm tired, so I'm stopping." They were commanded to work, work, work, and work until the job was finished and their master was satisfied.

When looking for the fittest soldiers, always look for those who are willing to go the second, third, and fourth mile to get the job done. Enlist soldiers who *stretch* themselves — *push* themselves — and make themselves keep going, even when the flesh screams "No!"

You must remember when waging war with the forces of hell, *endurance* is the name of the game! You have more power than the devil and more *authority* than the devil. No one can question this. Believers do not lose their fight in the combat zone because they don't have enough power or authority; *most believers lose their fight because they don't have enough endurance to stay in there and keep fighting!*

If you can endure, you'll win the race. Satan's tolerance for you will wear out. He'll recognize you have endurance. He'll know he can't beat you, and he'll leave. When he leaves, everything you've wanted and prayed for will come to you so quickly you'll call it a miracle! In reality, your "quick" miracle is not a miracle at all. Instead, understand that it is the result of your waiting, fighting, and enduring through it all! Had you given up earlier in the fight and not endured it all, your "quick" miracle would never have occurred!

Seventh, Vegetius says those who are accustomed to "digging trenches and carrying burdens" are best fit to the soldiers. Why? Because, like it or not, sometimes the load of ministry and warfare gets heavy. If we are wimpy and afraid to carry a little extra weight, we can kiss it all goodbye right now!

*In war, every soldier must know how to carry his own weight, and sometimes he is required to help carry the weight of others as well.*

All of these are essential qualities for good combat zone fighters. Peasants may not have been the "intellectuals" of their day, or members of the high-ranking aristocracy, but their hard-working existence in the field prepared them to be the best of fighters.

The upper crust of society — royalty, nobility, and the aristocracy — knew nothing of hardship, hard work, fatigue, unbearable heat, digging trenches, or carrying burdens. If a spade had been placed in their hands, they wouldn't have known what to do with it!

When you examine the believers of the Early Church, it is evident that they were not nobility. Instead, they were exactly the kind of people Vegetius describes: unspoiled by the luxuries of life, content with little, inured to fatigue, and accustomed to hard work. They were the very ones whom Paul called "faithful men." *They were, in fact, perfect soldiers!*

In First Corinthians 1:26-28, Paul says, "For ye see your calling, brethren, how that *not many wise men* after the flesh, *not many mighty, not many noble,* are called: But *God hath chosen the foolish things* of the world to confound the wise; and God hath chosen *the weak things* of the world to confound the things which are mighty; And *base things* of the world, and *things which are despised,* hath God chosen, yea, and *things which are not,* to bring to nought things that are."

Paul knew the background of the Roman army. He knew it was primarily composed of individuals with a peasant background: the poor, uneducated lower class. If it were not for the army, they would have remained peasants, poor and unimportant.

*However, those who were rejected by society turned out to make the best soldiers.* They knew how to fight!

Similarly, God has not called great masses from the nobility or the intellectuals into His army. He has called those whom the world would never have recognized. His army is made up of brave men and women who have committed their lives to a cause and now count as people who are very important.

In the Lord's army even someone who was once the lowest "scum" of society can be *transformed* into an important warrior!

As James puts it, "Hearken, my beloved brethren, Hath not God chosen *the poor* of this world rich in faith, and heirs of the kingdom which he hath promised to them that love him?" (James 2:5).

Vegetius said, "It is certain that the less a man is acquainted with the sweets of life, the less reason he has to be afraid of death."

People who have had to struggle in life often make the best combat zone fighters. They have *nothing to lose and everything to gain!* For them, the risk of failure is almost zero. In the world's eyes, they already are "failures." Now, with God's help, and no fear of hurting or losing their "reputation," they have *every reason* to answer the call of God and fight.

## The Cream of the Crop

At one point, Vegetius basically says, *"The rougher the background, the better the fighter."* In his official report, he says, "In choosing recruits regard should be given to their trade. Fishermen, fowlers, confectioners, weavers, and in general all whose professions more properly belong to women should, in my opinion, by no means be admitted into the service. On the contrary, smiths, carpenters, butchers, and huntsmen are the most proper to take into it."

So many times I've heard believers say, "Well, I really lived for the devil before I got saved. I don't think I'm the type that should be used very much. I've got a pretty rough background."

*Believe it or not, your rough background may just make you one of the best fighters!*

You may even say, "Well, by nature I was a real daredevil. I did a lot of bad things and made a lot of mistakes. I was a big sinner."

So what? Now you know the Lord. Take that same vigor you used to serve the devil, and use it now to serve the Lord. *You may be the cream of the crop!*

Vegetius said, "But what good can be expected from a man who is by nature a coward, though ever so well disciplined or though he has served ever so many campaigns?"

*Trained, educated, schooled men sometimes make the greatest cowards!* On many occasions, God has raised up *the profoundly uneducated* to do His will, because they were willing to take the risk!

Cowards will not do in the army of God, and if you are willing to fight, and have a past history of being a fighter, you may make one of the best fighters for the combat zone!

## The Best Age for Enlisting

Vegetius writes, "the proper time for enlisting youth into the army is at the age of puberty. At this time, instruction of every kind is more quickly absorbed and more lastingly imprinted on the mind. Besides this, the indispensable military exercises of running and leaping must be acquired before the limbs are too much stiffened by age. For it is this activity, improved by continual practice, which forms the useful and good soldier."

Again we see the difference in God's wisdom and ours. Man would say, "Leave the young boys at home. They are not ready for such instruction. They are too young to be used." This is yet another example of how God calls and chooses.

Perhaps this selection of young soldiers to do the work of ministry is nowhere more powerful than the selection of the twelve disciples by Jesus Himself. Why? *Because the oldest disciple Jesus called was no more than 27 years old, and it is agreed by most that the youngest of the twelve was possibly between 14 and 16 years old!*

Why? The Lord knew at this age, instruction was more quickly absorbed — the traditions of men had not yet set into their souls — and they were *young enough* and *bold enough* to take a leap of faith!

As Vegetius said, "the indispensable military exercises of running and leaping must be acquired before the limbs are too much stiffened by age. . ." Many people have been called, didn't respond, and later couldn't move on with God. Their spiritual limbs became too stiffened. Respond when God calls you!

This is why Paul said to Timothy, "Let no man despise thy youth. . ." (1 Timothy 4:12). This is why God could call a very young boy named Samuel, who may have been no older than 7 when "all Israel from Dan even to Beer-sheba knew that Samuel was established to be a prophet of the Lord" (1 Samuel 3:20).

Even the age of soldiers is different from what we would expect. *God will take any yielded person into His army!*

We must never forget the words of Job 32:6-9: "I am young in years, and you are old; that is why I was fearful, not daring to tell you what I know. I thought, 'Age should speak; advanced years should teach wisdom.' But it is the spirit in a man, the breath of the Almighty, that gives him understanding. It is not only the old who are wise, nor only the aged who understand what is right" *(New International Version).*

It is not years, nor age that counts in the army of God; rather, *it is a yielded vessel that God looks to use.* Even a young man or woman, because of the breath of the Almighty in his or her life, can be used as a fighter in God's combat zone!

## How To Train Good Soldiers

Vegetius writes, "We find that the Romans owed the conquest of the world to no other cause than continual military training, exact observance of discipline in their camps and unwearied cultivation of the other arts of war."

He continued, "They thoroughly understood the importance of hardening them [new recruits] by continual practice, and of training them to every maneuver in line and action. Nor were they less strict in punishing idleness and sloth."

You may be thinking, "That is incredible! They really expected a great deal out of their soldiers!" That is *exactly* the point!

Today, if we would harden ourselves to battle, go through continuous training, discipline, and were hard on idleness and slothfulness, our ranks would turn out different!

Instead, we pamper the saints, try not to hurt anyone's feelings, and do our best not to ask anything of them that will require extra effort on their part!

*Do you know what the problem is? The Church today is full of civilians, not soldiers!* We are attempting to affect a lost world without requiring much from the ranks! *We are supposed to be an army!*

Vegetius said, "No state can either be happy or secure that is amiss and negligent in the discipline of its troops."

The troops must be prepared, trained, and disciplined! Vegetius also said, "Numerous armies of raw and undisciplined troops are but masses of men dragged to slaughter."

Initial training of new recruits in the Roman army included: marching, leaping, swimming, sword practice, drill, and other forms of military exercises. All of these were *essentials.* In fact, the recruit could not receive the military mark (a permanent mark or "brand" imprinted on the hand of the soldier by a hot iron) *until* he had proven himself fit for service.

If he could not follow through in the exercises prescribed above, then he would not receive the "mark." This was true even if he had gone through all the exercises successfully but *one.* His lack of willingness to finish the test proved he was not fit for service.

Too often the Church has placed its official mark of approval on someone too soon. Because of outward appearance, or a past record in another church seems impressive, new arrivals to a local church are quickly elevated into positions of authority. Time and time again this results in *catastrophe!*

You must know your troops! If the person cannot survive training first, then he or she should not receive "the mark."

You ask, "What is the training?" If he or she cannot *submit,* does not *tithe,* does not *regularly attend,* cannot withhold his *judgmental opinion,* and so forth, he should never be formally announced as a combat zone fighter, or put in a position on the front lines.

If he or she cannot follow through on these basics, *why should you believe this person will remain true in the middle of a real challenge?* Let him or her simply be another number in the masses *until* the heart is softened and the soul is made ready, is tried, is proved, and is fit to be used.

This is why, in First Timothy 3:6, Paul said, "Not a novice, lest being lifted up with pride he fall into the condemnation of the devil." In First Timothy 5:22, he continues, "Lay hands suddenly on no man. . . ."

Concerning this, Vegetius says, "For many, although promising enough in appearance, are found unfit upon trial.

These are to be rejected and replaced by better men; for it is not numbers, but bravery which carries the day."

## Marching, Leaping, Swimming!

What a powerful statement Vegetius now makes! See if you agree with him: "...troops who march in an irregular and disorderly manner are always in great danger of being defeated."

This sounds like the Church in recent years, doesn't it? The troops have marched in an irregular and disorderly fashion, and it has certainly brought the devastating blows of the enemy against us.

We must understand what our place is, get in our place, stay there, and learn to march to the Lord's orders — without being threatened by someone else's more prominent place! *You cannot be everything!* Therefore, hear from God what your place is, get in it, march in order with the rest of God's army, and then we will do the enemy *great* harm!

In addition to marching, the soldiers were taught to *run, leap, and swim.* Vegetius said, "But the young recruits in particular must be exercised in running, in order to charge the enemy with vigor...leaping is another necessary exercise, to enable them to cross ditches or scale difficult eminences of any kind without trouble."

Charging the enemy and jumping ditches! Does that sound familiar to you? Have you ever had to charge the enemy? Have you ever had to jump some ditches? *This describes an aggressive and unrelenting faith!*

If you're a combat zone fighter, you know there are times when you must face the enemy — eyeball to eyeball — challenge him, and force him to move. Similarly, all combat zone fighters know at times that ditches — problems — seem to appear out of the blue! What are you going to do? That is when you face the stark reality that *faith is for jumping ditches or scaling impossible obstacles!*

Vegetius also mentions the exercise of *swimming.* He says, "Every young soldier, without exception, should be in the summer months taught to swim: for it is sometimes impossible to pass rivers on bridges, and the flying and pursuing army both are obliged to swim over them."

*This "swimming" reveals determination and sheer courage!* You may say this is a picture of "enduring hardness" to get the job done. It is interesting that Vegetius specifically said, "Every young soldier, without exception, should be in the summer months *taught to swim...*"

You ask, "Why is that so interesting?" Because it again tells us that *these skills do not come to most of us naturally.* We must be instructed, trained, and taught to obey the Lord in the midst of battle.

As Vegetius said, "Few men are born brave; but many become so through training and force of discipline."

*Few believers are born with tenacity and determination.* The flesh doesn't want to endure anything, pray about anything, do one thing extra, or deal with something that is difficult. The flesh must be subjected to a higher will, conquered, and then used for God's purposes.

This will only take place through constant and continual drill from the Holy Spirit! Do not take lightly the practice exercises He brings into your life. He is attempting to prepare you for a real battle!

## Be Sure To Go to Sword Practice

Because the Roman army was so committed to warfare, its soldiers practiced the arts of warfare *continually.* One primary and daily exercise was sword practice. They exercised themselves in this skill morning and afternoon.

The ancients gave their recruits bucklers that were woven with willow branches and were *two times heavier* than the ones used in actual battle. In addition, the swords they used in practice were made of heavy wood, and were *twice the weight of the real swords* used in battle.

Every soldier practiced combat with a wooden post about six feet high which was firmly fixed in the ground. This six-foot post became his "enemy" during practice. Just as with a real enemy, he would advance upon his target, strike hard with his sword, and then retreat.

His job in practice was to learn how to take advantage of his enemy; how to hit him at his weakest point; how to strike him so that he could not respond. His aim was nearly always pointed toward the head or face, at the thighs or legs, or occasionally at the sides of the target.

Vegetius says, "They were likewise taught not to cut, but to thrust with their swords. For the Romans not only made jest of those who fought with the edge of that weapon, but always found them *an easy conquest*. A stroke with the edges, though, made with ever so much force, seldom kills, as the vital parts of the body are defended both by the bones and armor. *On the contrary, a stab, although it penetrates but two inches, is generally fatal.*"

It was from this background that Paul said, "And take. . .the sword of the Spirit, which is the word of God" (Ephesians 6:17). How vital it is that we understand the sword of the Spirit!

Notice particularly Paul says, ". . .the sword of the Spirit, which is *the word of God.*" The word "word" is *not* the Greek word *logos* (lo-gos), which would refer to the written word. Instead, Paul employs the use of the Greek word *rhema* (rhe-ma). This is powerful!

Why?" you ask. Because had Paul used the word *logos* (the written Word), this would imply a "sweeping stroke" against the enemy, and this would never do.

The *logos* — although broad, heavy, wonderful and full of general direction for our lives — is not sufficient to give the enemy a fatal blow.

*We need to stab the enemy!*

This will require a *rhema,* or "a specific, quickened word" from the scripture, placed into our hearts and hands by the

Holy Spirit. With a *rhema* from God placed in our hearts and hands, then we have *"sword power!"* A genuine *rhema* does not have to be six pages long to be effective against the work of the devil.

Remember: All the Roman had to do was make *a two-inch penetration* into their enemies to kill them. *Likewise, one very small rhema from the Lord has power to do the adversary in!* Thank God for the sword of the Spirit!

The best example of this powerful sword of the Spirit is found in Luke 4:3-13. In this passage, Satan, like an aggressor, is found attacking Jesus on repeated occasions. Rather than simply saying, "Satan, get out of here, or my Father is going to get you," *Jesus stabs him repeatedly with direct blows!* Jesus had a specific, quickened *rhema* from the Spirit.

After tempting Jesus with food, Jesus drew the sword that the Spirit put in His hand (a *rhema*) and said, "It is written, That man shall not live by bread alone, but by every word of God" (v. 4). *To this stabbing sword of the Spirit, the enemy had no response.*

After offering Jesus all the kingdoms of the world in exchange for worship, *Satan was wounded deeply by one rhema from the mouth of Jesus.* Jesus said, ". . .it is written, Thou shalt worship the Lord thy God, and him only shalt thou serve" (v. 8). *To this sword of the Spirit, Satan had no answer.*

After tempting Jesus to prove His deity, Satan fled from the scene. *With one final stab, Jesus penetrated Satan's armor and nearly fatally wounded him.* Jesus answered him with *a sword!* He said, "It is said, Thou shalt not tempt the Lord thy God" (v. 12).

Like the Lord Jesus, when you are properly exercised with the sword of the Spirit, no battle is a real threat to you! Battles will cease to be a threat and will become *opportunities to prove your spiritual fitness!*

As Vegetius said, "A soldier perfected in his art. . .will be eager for an opportunity of distinguishing himself through the act of warfare."

## Spiritual Armaments

Paul often uses the analogy of Roman weaponry to describe our spiritual equipment. In Second Corinthians 10:4, he mentions our weapons when he says, "*The weapons of our warfare* are not carnal, but mighty through God. . . ." In Ephesians 6:11, he admonishes us to "Put on *the whole armour of God,* that ye may be able to stand against the wiles of the devil."

The weapons Paul keeps referring to are clearly from the picture of Roman soldiers dressed in full armor. This was an easy illustration for Paul to use, because he had been bound to such soldiers during many imprisonments.

Standing next to these illustrious soldiers, Paul could see the Roman soldier's *loin belt, huge breastplate, brutal shoes affixed with spikes, massive, full-length shield, intricate helmet, piercing sword, and long, specially tooled lance* which could be thrown a tremendous distance to hit the enemy from afar.

It is from this example that Paul received revelation about spiritual armor. Understand that these pieces of weaponry were not light; they were very, very heavy. Combined together, their total weight could exceed 100 pounds! Imagine how "fit" the soldier bearing these arms had to be in order to carry such equipment!

In the same manner, if you want to walk in full armor and function correctly in the combat zone, you must first be spiritually fit. Like the Roman soldier of New Testament times, *you must harden yourself to war by continual practice, obtain training in every possible maneuver against the enemy, and cut your flesh no slack at all.*

You may be asking, "All right, Rick, I understand. But how do I practice, and where does the practice take place?"

In your personal life and in the local church!

When the enemy comes against you because you've taken a stand on the Word, then it is time for you to fight.

Believe it or not, this may just be practice for the real fight still to come. Never take an opportunity to practice lightly!

Likewise, when the leadership of the local church asks for greater commitment from you, teaches you the Word, tells you to listen to teaching tapes, admonishes you to fight the enemy, come to intercession, stand on the Word, pray in faith, give of your finances, and devote yourself more deeply to the work of the Lord, understand that this is all practice!

That leadership is trying to get you ready for the real battle! Let them equip you, teach you, prepare you, and train you in every possible maneuver against the enemy.

You must be in the constant practice of warring, fighting, killing, and conquering in the spirit realm. You must go through constant drill, military exercises, hardship, and training — fully and regularly immersing yourself in all the disciplines that accompany warfare!

This constant, continual exercise and militaristic mindset will put you in a position to fight, outlast your enemy, and come out of the combat zone the winner — *the champion!*

So when Paul said, "No man that warreth. . . ." he was implying a great many things to his reader. He was likening our Christian commitment to the constant, continual, necessary exercise, discipline, and drill of the Roman soldier.

*Our primary occupation is to be at the business of "warring" and all that "warring" involves.* Because this is a present participle, it should be translated, "No man warring, warring, warring, and warring. . .," or "No man involved in constant combat. . .," or "No man serving as a full-time soldier. . . ."

## The Necessity of Carrying Burdens

Notice what Vegetius says about the load Roman soldiers had to carry. He says, "To accustom soldiers to carry burdens is also an essential part of discipline. Recruits in particular should be obliged frequently to carry a weight of not less than sixty pounds (not including his armor!), and to march with it in the ranks."

Then he tells us why this was so important: "This is because on difficult expeditions they often find themselves under the necessity of carrying their provisions as well as their arms."

Of course, our flesh never likes to do anything hard. However, we must come to grips with the bare facts: At times we must go the extra mile and bear the extra burden. Galatians 6:2 tells us, "Bear ye one another's burdens, and so fulfill the law of Christ." Just imagine: Those Roman soldiers were required to carry their own food, in addition to carrying all of their arms!

By preparing ourselves through constant training and mentally preparing ourselves to face and conquer the worst situations, we can do *anything* that is required of us. This is why Peter says in First Peter 1:13, "Wherefore, gird up the loins of your mind. . . ." We must keep our minds alert, prepared, and untangled from fear of hardness or challenge.

## God's Boot Camp

We must never say, "This is too hard," or withdraw when the heat of the challenge is turned up. We must get in boot camp and endure the hardness of subjecting our flesh to discipline. In our spiritual boot camp, the Church, our former titles, prestige, and worldly reputation cease to exist. We are stripped of our civilian clothes, have our heads shaved, are numbered, are given a new set of clothes, and are, for the time being, *just another soldier,* like all the rest.

Once enlisted by the Lord Himself, it no longer matters "who" you were in the world. Former titles are insignificant here. What counts is that you forget your past and your worldly success, throw yourself into your new lifestyle of training and combat, and become a *fit* soldier.

In God's boot camp, the Church, you are just another new soldier who needs to be trained, exercised, practiced, and disciplined until ready to fight.

You may say, "That doesn't make us sound very special! Rick, do you really mean we should view ourselves just as another number in God's army? Do you really mean this?"

Emphatically, *yes!*

To see yourself in this light, in no way removes God's special attention from your life. It does not make you "less than special." No, no, no! *You are special just to be enlisted by the Lord!* The fact that you are in His army, the Church, and have been enlisted by Him to fight, means you were handpicked — *chosen* — by Him. *You are very special!*

However, being specially *selected* by the Lord and specially *pampered* are two different things. And in order for us to become God's military ranks in these days, we must be willing to lay aside all past successes, titles, worldly ranks, and enter spiritual boot camp simply as another of many soldiers there to be trained, equipped, and sent forth. We must strip off our worldly garments, receive our number, and get in line to learn. *Boot camp is for beginners!*

I've often heard people say, "Our pastor is so hard on us! It seems like we finally come through a major, life-threatening crisis when suddenly — before you know it — we are being shoved back into another conflict!"

GOOD! It may seem difficult for the moment, but the constant, hard drill, the discipline, and the challenging lifestyle always make boys into great men of God and girls into great women of God. This is not bad. This is good!

I've heard other people say, "The pastor should really use So-and-so more than he does right now. Why, that person is a bank president." Or, "What is wrong with the leadership of our church? God has just sent us a concert pianist, and they are not using him!"

In time these people will be used. For now, however, let them be a *new recruit*. Let them strip off their former prestige, have their life shaved of former worldliness, be given a military number, put in line, disciplined, hardened through exercise, and then let them be used in the front lines.

If this was our philosophy, the Church today would be full of committed, driven, battle-fighting warriors rather than civilians with a "take-it-easy," "don't-make-it-too-hard," and "my-feelings-are-hurt" mentality.

We must allow our officers, the fivefold ministry gifts (apostles, prophets, evangelists, pastors, and teachers) to do what they are called to do! They are called to train us, teach us every necessary maneuver, and show us how to march in rank, how to step in order, how to take every possible advantage of the enemy, how to conquer the world, and then send us out to put our skills into practice.

Ministry and obeying God are not always easy. In addition to already difficult challenges, sometimes other loads are piled upon us. We have no choice except to bear the extra load and get the job done. *The difficulty of the task does not change the necessity of the task!* God needs someone to do the job.

## Staying Untangled From the World

Paul continues in Second Timothy 2:4, "No man that warreth entangleth himself with the affairs of this life. . . ." This means, "No man involved in constant combat. . .serving as a full-time soldier. . .warring, warring, warring, and warring. . . entangleth himself with the affairs of this life."

Especially pay heed to the word "entangleth." This word in Greek is the word *empleko* (em-ple-ko), which describes "a person entangled in his lower garments, or caught in some type of vine."

This word "entangleth" is the exact word used in Matthew 27:29 to describe Jesus' crown of thorns! It says, "And when they had *platted* a crown of thorns, they put it upon his head. . . ."

This may be the clearest example of the Greek word *empleko* that we have in the New Testament. How do you make a crown of thorns? You take vines that are filled with thorns and jagged ends and carefully *weave them together.* The different vines are so tightly *woven together* that they form a strong, secure circle, similar to the shape of a crown.

So when the Word says, "...they had *platted* a crown of thorns," it literally means, "They had *carefully woven together bunches of thorny vines* into a crown." This word "entangleth" describes "something that has been carefully woven together, like a woman who carefully weaves a garment."

By using this word "entangleth," Paul tells us committed, warring believers *do not* have the privileges of civilian life. The rewards will come, but they come later; not in the heat of the battle. In fact, *the real soldier does not have time to be consumed with the affairs of civilian life.*

To think constantly and habitually about life free from war does not change the war. Also, it almost always causes a soldier to be a lazy, uncommitted daydreamer who never gets his job done. To really have peace, you must be war-minded. As Vegetius said, "He, therefore, who aspires to peace should prepare for war."

Stop thinking about later, and start thinking about *right now!* It is wonderful to think about heaven. It is wonderful to think of relaxation and vacation. However, if bullets are flying all around you, you need to be paying attention to those bullets! *You are in the midst of warfare!* Win your battle and *then* rest and relax!

*Remember: You are living in the combat zone!*

## The Affairs of This Life

Paul answers our next question before we ask. Our question is: "What is it that we are supposed to stay free from? Does Paul mean, 'Stay free from money'? Does he mean, 'Stay free from your job'? Does he mean, 'Don't own a house'? Does he mean, 'Have no goals for your life'? What does Paul want us to stay untangled from?"

Paul answers our question: "No man that warreth entangleth himself with the affairs of this life. . ." (v. 4). The key to this verse is the word "affairs."

The word "affairs" is the Greek word *pragmeteia* (prag-me-teia), which refers to "a normal, regular daily regimen, or preoccupation with civilian life." It is where we get the word "pragmatic." It refers to practical things of normal life.

You could translate this, "No man serving as a full-time soldier, who is constantly fighting on the front lines of battle, who is warring, warring, and warring, has the privilege of allowing himself to be woven tightly together, or bound like ropes tied into a knot, with the normal preoccupations of civilian life. . ."

Why not? Because he is a soldier, *not* a civilian. Soldiers should not be concerned with the same things civilians are concerned with. Soldiers *must* have their minds on warfare! They must keep their minds on business at hand, or they may lose their lives!

Vegetius tells us this about temptations: "And if any long expedition is planned, they should be encamped as far as possible from the temptations of the city. By these precautions their minds, as well as their bodies, will properly be prepared for service."

Extra-long warring has a way of making you think hard about life without war! If camped too close to the city, so to speak, the lights, sounds, and aromas of the city may draw you off the battlefield and into the mainstream of civilian life.

Because soldiers had to maintain a constant militaristic mentality, they were not even permitted to *visit* the city! It was off-limits for them!

Likewise, we must draw the line between ourselves and preoccupation with civilian life. We cannot afford to sit idly by, thinking about how sweet civilian life is. That does not help you fight in the combat zone! You are a fighter, and you need to be concentrating on the job God gave you to do. *The devil is serious, and you'd better be serious, too.*

## How Was Timothy Tempted?

Paul did not chide Timothy for having a large house payment. He wasn't angry with Timothy for using credit cards, either. It is true that these things, when used wrong, can tie you up in a knot, take your attention off the combat zone, and get you sidetracked. If you abuse money, marriage, relationships, credit cards, material goods, and so on, it can bring about a deadly blow from the enemy.

While it is not wrong to have nice things, or to live in comfortable homes, *we must keep these things out of our hearts.*

It is possible to throw open the door, through abuse, materialism, or neglect, and invite the enemy to come right into our camp. While we have no choice but to deal with practical things in life, it is absolutely necessary for us *to keep them in our hands and out of our hearts.*

However, when Paul speaks of "the affairs of this life," he is *not* taking about material goods or possessions. Timothy wasn't tempted to be woven together with worldly things. No, this was the last thing on his mind. He had much greater problems to think about than house payments and car repairs.

Timothy's life was being threatened, and his church was declining. He was tempted to be interwoven with something, bound up tightly, like ropes tied into a knot.

What was Timothy tempted to be "entangled" with? *Self-preservation!*

## Like the Tentacles of an Octopus

What was trying to wrap itself around Timothy? Like the long tentacles of an octopus, *a spirit of fear* was reaching out to grab hold of Timothy, hold him in bondage, and suck the life out of him!

You see, for Timothy, *fear had become a part of his normal, regular, daily routine.* Like a civilian who is preoccupied with the affairs of bills, payments, car repairs, and so on, Timothy was preoccupied with what "might" happen to him if he were taken captive by Nero.

He was *consumed with fear* about making new leaders and being hurt by them, like the previous leaders had done. This fear was becoming *a regular part of his daily regimen!*

Fear was Timothy's biggest problem in life. It was *fear* that caused him to retreat from selecting new leaders. It was *fear* that was making him think twice about his relationship with Paul. It was fear that was making him think of "jumping ship" and forgetting about his walk with the Lord.

Have you ever been gripped with fear? Fear of failure! Fear of a lack of money! Fear of friends! Fear of success! Fear that you won't be able to handle success! Fear, fear, fear! Have you ever felt those long tentacles reach out to take you and hold you captive, sucking the life right out of you?

Just like Timothy, believers today still allow fear to wrap itself around them. When fear grabs hold, you can't even function or think!

Strong, overpowering fear can eventually lead you right down the path toward a nervous breakdown! The absolute truth is that fear will completely destroy you if you don't deal with it.

It starts with just one little fear; then it grows. It will keep expanding until you do something about it. It can begin anywhere. It can begin with a fear of finances. Then the fear of failure comes in. Then it moves beyond a fear of failure into something else.

By this time, fear has become so strong, you begin to feel a small ache in the body. Now you start having a fear of sickness. Then a fear of this, and a fear of that, and a fear of something else. Fear will crush you if you let it.

It doesn't make any difference that you have great aspirations for your life. If fear wraps itself around you, those aspirations are *on hold* until you conquer that fear.

There are times when fear has tried to grab hold of me. Like others, I have lain on my bed in the middle of the night and cried out to the Lord to deliver me from fear. I have had to deal with and overcome fear, too.

*Who is the author of fear? Satan.* Therefore, when fear comes on us, attempting to suffocate us and threaten our personal sanity, we must recognize it as an attack from Satan and resist it! We must tell it to "go" in Jesus' Name!

*Fear is a spiritual attack!*

Paul is telling Timothy (and us) all of this because he knows that if fear grabs hold of him (or us), we will not be able to please Jesus and complete the job the Lord gave us to do. When any believer walks in fear, he or she is like a walking time bomb, ready to explode at any minute, unstable and insecure.

If you desire to be a leader, or if you are already a leader in the Church, you must make the decision *to get rid of fear.* You are a soldier, and *you do not have the privilege of fear!*

## Take the "Big Leap"

Joshua certainly must have had to deal with fear. He was a great, anointed leader, but he was also a man. How do you suppose Joshua felt when God said to him, ". . . now therefore arise, go over this Jordan . . ." (Joshua 1:2).

What God told him to do was a most difficult thing! It was harvest time, and the Jordan River was flowing out of its banks. It was flood time! And God said, "Now you arise — thou and all the people. Come on, I want you to take *the big leap!*"

Joshua's reply could have been, "Now, Lord, don't You know that this is flood time?" But God made His message to Joshua clear: "Just put your feet into the water. When you dip your feet into the water, the water will part for you, and you and your people will walk across on dry ground."

The easy part was hearing God's command — that's always the easy part. The real challenge is when you step out *to do* what God said! It is putting your foot into the water that is the hard part; especially if you have already announced to everyone that the water is going to part!

*What if it doesn't part?* Yes, you're right — you'll look like an absolute fool.

Every leader and believer is faced with this same prospect. *What if it doesn't part? What if it doesn't work?* Anytime God tells you to do something, you can be sure, fear will try to come and say, "*What if, what if, what if...*" If you have not already dealt with this, you are the exception to the rule.

We all have the opportunity to become totally preoccupied with what God *can't* do — what *may* happen — all kinds of questions — and *totally miss* what God has in store for us to do!

In light of all this, Paul says, "No man serving as a full-time soldier, who lives in constant combat, who is warring, warring, and warring, has the privilege of letting the nitty-gritty affairs of life get him down... *A real combat zone fighter has no time to be preoccupied with affairs other than warfare.*"

## A Personal Goal for Every Soldier

Paul continues in verse 4, "No man that warreth entangleth himself with the affairs of this life; that he may *please* him who hath chosen him to be a soldier."

Particularly pay heed to the phrase, "that he may *please* him...." Now Paul begins to describe what our greatest desire in life should be. He tells us what every real combat zone fighter must aspire for in life. He says our goal should be that we may "please him that hath chosen him to be a soldier."

The word "please" is the Greek word *aresko,* (a-re-sko), which always conveys the idea of something that is "virtuous, delightful, fit, perfect, or pleasing." It was used once in classical Greek to describe horses that were trained, swift, beautifully proportioned, and a pleasure to watch perform. They were superb horses.

By using this word, Paul tells us what our chief desire should be. All of this training, while it will help us win our personal battles, will make us into the kind of Christians that God loves to watch perform!

Our whole goal and purpose should be to become so developed, so fit, so trained and prepared, that the Lord will enjoy watching us do our warfare!

Would the Lord get pleasure watching the way you fight right now? Would He see you as one who is trained, prepared, and fit for service? We decide what God sees. It is up to us to determine what type of soldier we will be.

## Who Is Your Enlisting Officer?

Notice the next phrase, where Paul says, "...that he may please *him who hath chosen him to be a soldier.*"

The phrase "who hath chosen him to be a soldier" is also very significant. This entire phrase is from the Greek word *stratologosanti* (stra-to-lo-go-san-ti). It refers to the top-ranking officer who enlisted all the new recruits into the military.

By using this word, Paul tells us that Jesus Christ, our Enlisting Officer, carefully chose us to be in His army; He called us forth, conscripted us into His service; and is now our Commanding Officer!

When you come to the end of this verse, it is almost as though Paul says, "Your chief concern should be to make sure your Commanding Officer, the One who chose you, called you, and conscripted you into service, finds you well trained and fit."

The Lord, our Commanding Officer, will take full responsibility to provide our needed provisions and food. As a Commanding Officer, we are His responsibility. Famine will not occur under His great care; neither will He allow disease to attack the ranks.

He will faithfully fulfill all His duties as the Commanding Officer. Whatever you need to fight better, He will provide to you *freely.*

However, with all His faithfulness and provisions, He cannot make you train, prepare, and become ready for the fight. He can send equippers and trainers into our midst, but He can't make us obey them and submit to their authority.

Paul says, "Timothy, the Lord is our Commanding Officer. He will provide everything you need to come out of this combat zone the winner! However, you must make the decision to be a good soldier. He can't make this decision for you.

"Make it your aim in life to become trained, prepared, and fit to serve in the Lord's army. Make the Lord's personal satisfaction your highest aim. Remember: To please your Enlisting Officer is your most important business. Do whatever is required to accomplish this feat."

## Final Word About the King's Army

In this chapter, we have seen what God expects from His army. We, the Church, must recognize we are called to be more than pew-warmers, and *we must come to grips with the reality of warfare.*

It is time for us to move out of our comfort zone and into the combat zone to which He called us — to fight, to wage war, to drive back the foes of hell.

Never again let us say we are too tired, too weary, or too handicapped to obey our Commanding Officer. If we decide to fall in line, get in rank, and march in an orderly fashion, He will provide everything else we need.

*This is the day of the militant believer!*

Let us rise with the weapons and power of God in our hands to do service for our King!

*This is an hour of confrontation!*

In the next chapter, we will see how Paul switches from the illustration of a soldier to the illustration of an athlete. To compete in this game of life called "the combat zone," it is essential that you prepare and become fit!

Your competitor, the devil, is ready to take you on in the wrestling ring, ready to fight it out in a boxing match, and ready to pin you to the mat in defeat.

Only a decision — *made by you* — to prepare for the fight will put you in a position to win this strategic fight for life!

## Chapter 7
# Training for the Combat Zone

Suddenly, the military talk stops, and Paul picks up a different picture to convey more ideas of commitment, warring, fighting, determination, skill, drill, and discipline — traits that are absolutely necessary to win a war in the combat zone.

In Second Timothy 2:5, Paul says, "And if a man also strive for masteries, yet is he not crowned, except he strive lawfully." Paul now begins using the illustration of *a professional athlete.*

The word "strive" is from the Greek word *athlesis* (ath-le-sis), which always described a man who was involved in *tremendous athletic competition.*

At the time of this writing, like today, there were both amateur and professional athletes. If you were an amateur, you were not considered to be a very serious contender. If you were a professional, however, it was said that you were an athlete who was "striving for the mastery."

This kind of athlete was going for the very top — the mastery — of his profession. This man was determined to be the absolute best. There was not an amateur bone in them; they were totally committed. It is this very word, *athlesis,* that describes committed, full-time, professional athletes, which Paul now uses in his letter to Timothy.

Remember, in Second Timothy 2:3,4, Paul has already told Timothy to endure hardness as a good soldier of Jesus

Christ; to be in the habit of warring, fighting, and preparing himself for combat.

Timothy now knows he must become everything *in the spirit* that a Roman soldier was *in the natural* — fierce, at times hard, meaner than the adversary, trained, committed, accustomed to bad climate and exposure to the heat, able to carry his own weight, and even able to carry others if need be, trained in every possible maneuver against the enemy, trained in every available weapon, and accustomed to particularly long and tedious expeditions.

Paul now switches to the illustration of athletics, making a strong, strong statement which confronts Timothy (and us) with a very important question. By saying "striving for masteries," he is asking Timothy to come to grips with a decision.

## Amateurs or Professionals?

Paul means to make Timothy (and us) face this decision:

(1) Are you serving the Lord just for fun; that is, *are you an amateur* who isn't really committed to go all the way, and who is just serving the Lord because it is popular, convenient, and fun to do right now for the moment?

Or, (2) *Are you a professional* — willing to pay any price; willing to undergo any kind of preparation; willing to work hard, bear up under pressure, and endure it all until you come out the winner?

*Are you really committed?*

We must ask ourselves these same questions. It is fun to serve the Lord, to be a part of the local church, tithe, give offerings, attend meetings, pray, and sing together when there are no problems and it basically costs us nothing.

However, if things change and it becomes challenging to serve the Lord, if problems emerge in your local church, or if the devil attacks your finances, making it difficult to give your tithes and offerings, what are you going to do? Will you still serve the Lord? Will you still be faithful to your local church? Will you still tithe and give offerings?

The question for all of us is: *"Are we amateurs, or are we professionals?"*

## Rules Are the Same for Each Competitor

Look at Paul's statement in Second Timothy 2:5. He says, "And if a man also strive for masteries. . . ." Particularly notice the word "man," because this is the Greek word *tis*. The word *tis* would be better translated "anyone." The idea of this word is "anyone at all."

This tells us two important things. First, *anyone* can register in the Lord's army and be counted to compete in the fight of faith if he or she desires. This verse is for *tis* — "anyone." Second, it tells us that anyone who decides to be a competitor had better pay heed to proper preparation and training.

*The mastery is not attained without great effort.* Yes, anyone can enlist, but no one can win the challenge unless he does it correctly. *The rules are the same for each competitor.*

That is why Paul continues to say, "And if a man also strive for masteries, yet is he not crowned, except he strive *lawfully.*"

The word "lawfully" doesn't really refer to the rules of the game, but to *the standard of training and preparation* every professional athlete went through *before the game* actually started.

This is important. It tells us we should never attempt to enter the real arena until we have gone through the necessary preparation to win. If you enter the arena without preparation, you'd better be ready to spend some time recuperating in intensive care, because you will not win! *Winners are those who have trained and prepared themselves.*

## The High Privilege of Being a Competitor

Then, as now, they had athletic "scouts." These scouts would go out into the communities to look over all the young athletes. Athletics was a big thing among the Greeks. In fact, those who won the competitions were adored and worshipped. The main goal of the Greeks was to find the most fit athletes to compete in the games.

After finding a "fit" athlete, the scout would issue him or her an invitation to training camp. The athletes were not forced to attend. It was considered a high privilege to be personally invited to become a professional athlete.

At camp, they were introduced to body-builders, trainers, and others skilled at fighting and competition. They were put on a rigid diet and exercise program. The trainers would put them through incredible routines to build both the body and the mind, for it was deemed equally important to be mentally alert as well as physically fit.

This training was serious. In fact, if you broke your diet more than once, you were kicked out of training camp and forbidden to participate in professional athletics again. In other words, if you broke your diet to eat one great, greasy fast-food hamburger, that was it — you were gone!

Timothy knew all about these things. Everyone knew about athletes and the strict, regimented training athletes went through *just in order to compete.* It didn't require much thinking for Timothy to understand all the connotations of Paul's statement about "striving for the masteries." He knew immediately what Paul was inferring.

But can you imagine what Timothy must have been thinking to himself by this time? Just when Timothy is about to catch on to Paul's instructions to be a *soldier,* Paul dramatically switches illustration, and seems to say, "Oh, forget the solder thing, and be an *athlete* instead!"

Then, in Second Timothy 2:6, Paul switches illustrations for a third time! He says, "The husbandman that laboureth. . . ." Paul begins talking about a *farmer!* Whoa!

Timothy must have thought, "What in the world is Paul talking about? He tells me to be a soldier, then an athlete, and now a farmer!"

## Three Important Points

Paul is making three important points. They are:

*(1) You'd better have the commitment of a soldier,* because you are going to be out on the front lines. Sometimes it is going to be tough. You have no choice, however. You are called to live and fight in the combat zone. (See Chapter 6 for a detailed look at soldiers.)

*(2) You'd better make the commitment to prepare like an athlete.* Athletes don't just get up one day and decide to try fighting in the ring! They are in constant training and preparation of the most difficult kind.

The mistake many Spirit-filled people make is, they think that once you are filled with the Holy Spirit, you don't need to think, use your mind, or do any type of normal, natural preparation. This is error! We must understand that we have been called of the Holy Spirit to train and prepare. *If we do not respond properly, we will not be used!*

The Holy Spirit "scouted out" the world. He found some of us who looked like we had potential. He invited us to "training camp," with a personal invitation of the Gospel, and we responded. When we said "yes" to the Gospel message, He brought us and plopped us right down in a training camp that is called "THE CHURCH."

In the Church, there are all kinds of trainers and body-builders. They are called: "apostles, prophets, evangelists, pastors, and teachers." These professional trainers are supernaturally gifted and equipped to put meat on you and get that meat in good shape!

They know exactly how to put you on a diet of the Word — the correct diet — and just how much of which ingredients you need. They are also skilled when it comes to the subject of making you use your faith and spiritually exercise.

*Your part is to listen to them!*

Leadership begins in the local church. If you will be faithful in the local church, if you will allow God to train you there, if pastors and ministry gifts have the opportunity to work on you and work you over, then you will be trained, prepared, and ready for any fight that comes along!

If you "strive lawfully" — if you go through all these necessary precautions and preparations — you will be ready for the real challenge, and ultimately you will be "crowned." I don't know about you, but I *love* prizes! The prizes back in those days were outstanding! However, we will get to this a little later on in this chapter.

Paul gives one last illustration in this chapter:

*3. You'd better be hard working, like a farmer!* Whew! He has gone from a soldier to an athlete and now to a farmer! We will put this third point, the farmer illustration, on hold until we get back to it again in Chapter 8. For now, let's continue in the vein of verse 5, where Paul talks about "striving for the masteries."

## Exercise While Stark Naked

Keep in mind, Paul is using athletic language in verse 5. He is telling us to prepare, train, and be equipped — then we will be able to win the fight!

Paul uses this athletic language throughout the New Testament. One powerful example is from First Timothy 4:7, where Paul says, "But refuse profane and old wives' fables, and *exercise thyself* rather unto godliness." This particular word for "exercise" gives us tremendous insight into Paul's thinking.

The word "exercise" is the Greek word *gumnadzo* (gum-nad-zo), and literally means "exercise while stark naked, or exercise while in the nude."

Now what does that mean? To our minds, this sounds ridiculous and makes no sense. But Timothy knew exactly what this word meant, because he was from a Greek world.

This was a word used only to describe *professional athletes.* By using this word, Paul is conveying a message to Timothy which is absolutely clear.

Timothy probably did not want to hear it, however. Remember, he had been working extremely hard in First Timothy, was physically exhausted, and wanted to take a break. Instead of encouraging him to take it easy, sit back, and take a break, Paul admonishes him to "exercise"; that is, *strip off all your clothes — strip until you are stark naked — and then get to work — harder, harder, and harder!*

"What does all this mean?" Take special notice of this word *gumnadzo,* because it was used to describe athletes in training for *combat sports.* Specifically, it described the manner in which athletes and competitors prepared and trained to fight.

There were primarily three forms of combat sports: *boxing, wrestling, and pankratists.* All of these sporting events were done in the nude.

It is important that Paul uses this *combat sports* word. In all the verses we studied so far, he has been talking about training, skill, discipline, work, and endurance. Now he continues talking about how to get ready to fight in the combat zone, but he also begins using a strange, *barbaric* form of illustration — that of *the boxer, the wrestler, and the pankratist.*

## Boxing: The Most Barbaric Sport of All

You say, "Why do you call these sports strange and *barbaric?*"

First, their boxers were not like ours today. Theirs were *extremely violent* — so violent that they were not permitted to box without wearing helmets. Without the protection of helmets, their heads would have been crushed.

Few boxers in the ancient world ever lived to retire from their profession. Most of them died in the ring. Of all the sports, the ancients viewed boxing as *the most* hazardous and deadly.

In fact, these boxers were so brutal and barbaric, they wore gloves that were *ribbed with steel and spiked with nails!* At times the steel wrapped around their gloves was *serrated,* like a hunting knife, in order to make deep gashes in the skin of an opponent.

In addition to this, boxers began using gloves that were heavier and much more damaging. It is quite usual, when viewing artwork from the time of the early Greeks, to see boxers whose faces, ears, and noses were totally deformed because of these dangerous gloves.

In studying the art of the Greeks, it is also quite usual to see paintings of boxers with blood pouring from their noses and with deep lacerations on their faces as a result of the serrated metal and spiked nails on the gloves. And it was not unusual for a boxer to hit the face so hard, with his thumb extended toward the eyes, that it knocked an eye right out of its socket.

Believe it or not, even though this sport was so combative and violent, there were *no rules* — except you could not clench your opponent's fist. That was the only rule of the game! There were no "rounds" like there are in boxing today. The fight just went on and on and on until one of the two *surrendered* or *died* in the ring.

This sport, like the others in that day, was done with no clothing on. The athletes desired total freedom of movement, and they believed that clothing would severely restrict their boxing. Not only that, but it was too easy for an opponent to grab hold of your clothing in order to toss you to the ground. Therefore, *clothing was out!*

However, this left every part of their body exposed to attack, and any part of the body was game. Remember: There were no rules when it came to boxing.

An inscription from the first century said of boxing: "A boxer's victory is obtained through blood." This was a thoroughly violent sport.

Then there was *wresting.*

## The Bone-Breaking, Back-Snapping, Blood-Spilling Sport

Wrestling was deeply loved by the Greeks and Romans alike. Although the description you are about to read is gruesome and full of bone-breaking, back-snapping, blood-spilling examples, it was the *least* injurious of all the combat sports.

This sport was so adored that in Greece, you were not really considered an *educated* man until you had become an avid wrestler yourself. This sport required much of you — self-reliance, endurance, boldness, craftiness, and courage. These were virtues every Greek aspired to possess. They were readily obtained and maintained in the sport of wrestling.

Wrestlers, too, often wrestled to the death. In fact, a favorite tactic in those days was to grab hold of an opponent around the waist from behind, throw him up in the air, and quickly break his backbone in half from behind. In order to make an opponent surrender, it was quite normal to strangle him into submission. Choking was another acceptable practice. So wrestling was another extremely violent sport.

They were tolerant of every imaginable tactic: *breaking fingers, breaking ribs by a waistlock, gouging the face, knocking eyes out, and so forth*. Although less injurious than the other combat sports, wrestling was still a bitter struggle to the end.

In fact, nearly all the art of the early Greeks reveals Greek wrestlers with huge blood prints left all over their bodies from the fight. Wrestling was a bloody, bloody sport.

Although it is difficult to believe, the contemporary television program "Championship Wrestling" is very similar to the way the early Greeks wrestled — except, "Championship Wrestling" would not be considered *violent enough* by the Greeks' standards!

Then there were *pankratists*.

## Supreme Power Over All

*Pankratists* were a combination of all of the above. The word *pankratists* is from two Greek roots, the words *pan* and *kratos*. *Pan* means "all," and *kratos* is a word for "exhibited power." The two words together describe *someone with massive amounts of power; power over all; more power than anyone else.*

This, indeed, was the purpose of *Pankration*. Its competitors were out to prove they could not be beaten and were tougher than anyone else!

In order to prove this, they were permitted to kick, punch, bite, gouge, strike, break fingers, break legs, and do any other horrible thing you could imagine!

Once again, they fought in the nude, because their opponent could grab hold of an article of their clothing in order to toss them to the ground. This naked condition was especially serious to this sport where kicking was allowed. There was no part of the body that was off-limits. They could do anything to any part of their competitor's body, for *there were basically no rules.*

An early inscription says this about *Pankration:* "If you should hear that your son has died, believe it, but if you hear he has been defeated, do not believe it." More died in this sport than surrendered or were defeated. Like the other combat sports, it was *extremely violent*.

## What Does "Strive Lawfully" Really Mean?

Paul's statement to Timothy in Second Timothy 2:5, "...yet is he not crowned, except he strive lawfully," is tremendously misunderstood by many people, including good Bible teachers.

People have read it to say, "That's right! If you want to win, then you must compete according to the rules while you are fighting. If you fight according to the rule book, the Bible, you will win!"

I used to read and teach it this way, and it is true that you must fight and stand on God's Word. However, history will not support this verse and statement to be about that. It reveals something very different about the phrase "strive lawfully."

You must understand what Paul is saying. The word "lawfully" refers only to the preparation *before the fight*. You see, there were no rules *during* the fight. No rules! Understand, there were basically no rules at all in these combat sports. It was every man for himself!

Paul's exhortation is, "Prepare yourself." Go through the necessary training and regimen "lawfully" — the necessary routine, exercises, training, and preparation — *before the battle begins,* because once it begins, there are no rules, and there is no time for preparation.

This is a fight where anything goes. You'd better prepare, train, and get ready for it in advance. The word "lawfully" speaks of training and preparing *before the fight begins!*

## Wresting With Principalities and Powers

Paul uses the word "wrestle" in Ephesians 6:12. He says, "For we wrestle not against flesh and blood, but against principalities, against powers, against the rulers of the darkness of this world, against spiritual wickedness in high places."

By using this word "wrestle," which is the old Greek word *pale,* Paul conveys the idea of *a bitter struggle and an intense conflict* — which describes our warfare with demonic forces as a combat sport!

This means when you are fighting demonic foes, *there are no rules! Anything goes!* All methods of attack are legal, and there is no umpire to cry "foul" when the adversary attempts to break you, choke you, or strangle you.

*Whoever fights the hardest, the meanest, and lasts the longest is the winner of this confrontation.* Therefore, you'd better be equipped, alert, and prepared before the fight begins.

## A Place of Struggle and Conflict

The athletes prepared for their combat sports in a building called the *Palastra*. The name *Palastra* comes from the Greek word *pale*, which describes "a struggle or bitter conflict." Therefore, this name *Palastra* really means "a house of struggle."

The *Palastra* was normally a huge building that resembled a palace; really, it was a palace of combat sports, dedicated to the cultivation of athletic skills. Here you could find professional athletes: boxers, wrestlers, *pankratists*, and so on.

Nearly every hour of the day and night, this building was filled to overflowing with those who were dedicated to their skill; those who were "striving for the mastery." It was filled with trainers, equippers, and experts at fighting.

*The Palastra is a type of the Church!* Everything the athlete needed to get ready to fight — all the knowledge and equipment needed — could be obtained by the athlete inside the *Palastra*.

The *Palastra* was full of exercise equipment, weapons, and athletic equipment, body-builders and weights, and so forth. Everything an athlete needed to prepare and train was there, if he would only take advantage of it.

Likewise, the Church is a huge and wonderful "palace" where Christian soldiers are being prepared to fight like soldiers or compete like athletes. Everything the believer needs to prepare himself for the fight — Bible knowledge, training, gifts of the Spirit, patience, faith, and so on — is right there inside the Church, if he or she decides to take advantage of it.

Inside the Church, you can receive everything you need in order to fight a good fight! *Everything!*

## The Undressing Room

When a competitor or an athlete would come into the *Palastra*, the first thing that would happen is they would take him into a room called the *apoduterion* (apo-du-te-rion), which was an "undressing room."

In this room, the athlete would strip stark naked. While it was an undressing room, it was not a typical locker room. It was really a "preparation room."

In the middle of the *apoduterion* were huge, hot, steamy baths. In another section of the room were huge slabs of stone and marble which looked like tables made out of marble.

It was here, in this undressing room, that the athlete began his work of preparation by undressing, bathing, cleansing himself, and lying atop the tables, first on his stomach, and then on his back, as his trainer rubbed *the first application of oil* into his muscles and flesh.

Often, amateur athletes would venture into the *Palastra* to read the daily docket in order to find out who their competitors were that day. If the competition looked too fierce, many would turn away and return home. They were not really committed athletes and fighters.

But those who read the list and then stripped off all their garments, were committed to fight! The act of shedding one's garments was itself a statement: "I am here to the end. I am going to endure this thing. I am going to go through the process of preparation, because I intend to fight."

## It Is Time To Strip Your Clothes Off

In the *apoduterion,* the "undressing room," the committed contender started his vital work of preparation. Once undressed, he went straight toward the baths to cleanse himself thoroughly. Then, after he completed undressing, bathing, cleansing, and receiving the first application of oil rubbed into his flesh by his trainer, he was ready to go into the next room, the *aleiplerion* (a-lei-plerion), a room that maintained a perfect temperature for *the second heavy application of oil.*

If the *Palastra* is a type of the Church, then we must consider the prerequisites of the *apoduterion,* the undressing room.

If the *Palastra* is a type of the Church, this means we cannot go for the second, heavy application of oil *until we have received the first.*

Let's look at the activities of the *apoduterion,* the undressing room, to see what God requires of us before we receive an extra-heavy-duty anointing of the Spirit. First, we must ask, "What does the removal of clothes represent in the believer's life?"

Often in scripture, the removal of sin, evil, and wrong attitudes is likened to the removal of old, soiled, and unwanted clothes. Sin and wrong attitudes must be dealt with like old clothes: They must be taken off, laid down, pushed aside, and put away forever.

For instance, First Peter 2:1 says, "Wherefore, *laying aside* all malice, and all guile, and hypocrisies, and envies, and all evil speakings. . . ."

The phrase "laying aside" is from the Greek word *apotithimi* (apo-ti-thi-mi), which was used in a classical sense to denote the removal of an old set of clothes. By using the word *apotithimi,* Peter literally means, "Wherefore, remove these attitudes from your life *as if they were an old set of unwanted clothes. . .*"

James 1:21 says, "Wherefore *lay apart* all filthiness and superfluity or naughtiness. . . ."

This phrase "lay apart" is the same Greek word *apotithimi,* which tells us James means, "Wherefore, *take off, lay down, and push away forever like an old set of clothes,* the filthiness, and evil excess in your lives. . ."

Ephesians 4:22 says, "That ye *put off* concerning the former conversation the old man. . . ."

The phrase "put off" is also the Greek word *apotithimi*. Paul means, "Like an old set of clothes that need to be taken off, pushed aside, and discarded, take off your old man and throw him away. . ."

Colossians 3:9 indicates the same thing: "Lie not one to another, seeing that ye have *put off* the old man with his deeds."

This phrase "put off" is also the Greek word *apotithimi*. It once again likens the removal of sin and bad attitudes to the removal of one's clothes.

If the *Palastra* is a type of the Church (which it is), this means the true, committed contender — the believer who really wants to fight and compete in the combat zone — must *first* make a decision to strip some things off and out of his life. In fact, there can be no bathing, cleansing, and anointing until these appendages are removed from our lives.

Laziness, slothfulness, hurt, anger, fear, resentment, animosity, grudges — all of these must be *stripped off* of us like an old set of clothes to be discarded forever.

The athlete of the *Palastra* could not receive any application of oil until his clothes were *first removed*.

How in this world do we believe we are going to have a great anointing of the Spirit in our lives when we carry wrong attitudes, anger, resentment, fear, and other such baggage around with us? If we are really serious contenders — if we truly want to fight and win in the combat zone — we must go through the same process of preparation.

Step number one is: We must strip off all bondages, appendages, and excess weight out of our lives. If we do not remove all this undesirable baggage, there will be no first or second application of the Holy Spirit's oil in our lives.

*The oil belongs to those who strip off all hindrances and now stand totally yielded, submitted, and naked before God.*

Have you properly prepared yourself to receive the first application of the Spirit's oil for your life?

After making the decision to go all the way as a genuine contender in this fight of faith, we must visit the hot, steamy baths of cleansing water to remove any residual left behind. We must allow the blood of Jesus and the cleansing water of the Word to remove any speck or hindrance still remaining.

Like the athletes of old, we must dip into the hot, steamy, cleansing water to come up squeaky clean! *Our cleansing waters are the combined work of the blood and the Word!*

Then we'll be ready for that first dose of oil — *but not until!*

## The First Dose of Oil

If an athlete was willing to do all this; that is, strip off all his clothes, bathe and cleanse himself, then he was taken from the baths directly to the large, marble slabs, to lie down on his stomach, so his trainer could begin applying the first application of oil. You could not receive this first application until you were naked, bathed, and cleansed. *There were no shortcuts in this important procedure.*

This is vital. Remember, the *Palastra* is a type of the Church. Timothy immediately thought of all these things when Paul mentioned the word "exercise," the Greek word *gumnadzo,* which means "exercise while naked." He and all of his contemporaries were well acquainted with the activities of committed, naked athletes and the rigorous manner in which they trained and prepared for their competitions.

Before you receive your first vital application of oil, spiritually speaking, you must *decide* whether or not you are really a serious contender.

Are you going to be like others, who read the list and find out the competition is fierce, and then walk out? And if you are willing to fight, are you willing to strip yourself of every wrong attitude, laziness, slothfulness, animosity, grudges, and fear?

Are you willing to keep going on, and to keep on fighting, even if the odds are against you?

If so, are you willing to bathe and cleanse yourself before the first application of oil? Are you willing to turn from these wrong attitudes and emotions, sin and filth from the past, and leave the world behind, so the first application can be applied?

This is absolutely necessary if you want to move on with God. *Without this,* you will never be taken down the hall into the next chamber for the second, heavy-duty application of the Spirit's oil in your life.

## Once Naked, the Oil Is Applied

Once the athlete had done all that was necessary to receive his first application of oil, the trainer would come into the *apoduterion,* the undressing room, to the large marble slab where the athlete was lying.

Carrying a huge basin which was filled to the top with expensive rubbing oil, the trainer would begin to rub the oil into the skin of the athlete.

Sometimes it would take hours to do this job. The trainer's job was to rub that oil in, pressing it harder and harder, until the skin was soft, smooth, supple, and the muscles were toned and in good shape.

The trainer would rub, rub, and rub that oil until it was completely pressed into the athlete's skin. This wasn't a normal body rub, either. Because the trainer wanted to press it deep into the skin, at times this rubdown was painful, as he dug his fingers and hands deep and hard into the athlete's flesh. *It was a thorough workover.*

Once the skin was saturated with oil, and all the pores of the skin were clogged with oil, so that dirt and grime could not penetrate them during the fight, the athlete was made ready for his second, heavy-duty application of oil. However, a period of rest and relaxation was required before he could move on into the next anointing chamber.

Likewise, God often allows us a break, a period of time, to lapse between each new anointing in our life. If we received all of the anointings of God too quickly, just like the Greek athlete of old, it would be too much for our bodies. Therefore, *God allows us a rest as we leave one dimension of the anointing and prepare to enter into the next.*

## A Spiritual Picture

*This first application of oil* is a beautiful picture of our spiritual lives.

The first application of the Spirit's anointing *will* be applied to our lives if we are willing to strip ourselves of all "bulk weight" (wrong attitudes, wrong motives, laziness, fear, and so forth); if we are willing to bathe in the cleansing water of the blood and the Word; if we are willing to come into the Church, totally yield ourselves, submit ourselves, and open our hearts to the work of a pastor, or overseer, of the local church; and if we are willing to allow that pastor to tone us with the Word and give us a real, challenging workover.

A pastor is a perfect example of the trainer of the *Palastra,* who was also called "the manager of the *Palastra.*" We must permit our local pastor, like the trainer or manager of the *Palastra,* to give us a thorough workover. We must allow our trainer to press the first application of the oil hard into our lives until we are saturated with the Word and the oil.

*We must allow the pastoral gift to press the Word hard and deep into our lives, even when it is painful to bear, filling up the pores of our life so we will not pick up wrong attitudes, bitterness, and fear when we actually begin to engage in the battle.*

Then, after this vital work of preparation is done, we will be in a position to receive *the second application* of the Spirit's oil in our lives. However, if we are not willing to start here, we can forget the second application of the Spirit's oil and greater anointing.

It is the second application that everyone seems to seek. But you must know this: *It is not possible to have the second until you have received the first.* This was not permitted for athletes in the *Palastra,* and neither does God permit it in the Church. *There are no shortcuts in God!*

## First Things First

Some may say, "That's legalism!" No, you're wrong. It isn't legalism at all.

You say, "Give me proof!"

Let's look at Paul's words in Second Corinthians 1:21: "Now he which stablisheth us with you in Christ, and hath anointed us, is God."

You say, "What's so great about that verse?"

Look at *the order!*

Paul says, "Now he which stablisheth us. . . ." Before there is any mention of the anointing, Paul first mentions being "established."

You see, we want to get ahead of things sometimes. We want to dash right into the greatest anointing, the greatest power, and the greatest ministry. But it simply doesn't happen this way with God! God will require you to be "established" first.

*Really, this is the primary problem with many ministries today.* They have been elevated by man too quickly, promoted too fast, and have not been "established" long enough in the Lord to have the proper maturity to deal with their new notoriety. This is why so many of them have fallen into sin, financial indiscretion, and so on.

God desires that we be "established" first. This does not mean that God is trying to put the brakes on you; rather, God is trying to *prepare* you, *train* you, and *establish* you first. The anointing of the Spirit is precious to God. If you want to receive a greater anointing and handle it correctly, then get first things first. First, you must become established.

You ask, "Renner, what do you mean by 'established'?"

I'm talking about such extremely basic things as: church membership, faithfulness, becoming a faithful tither, becoming a church worker, being dedicated to the Word, attempting to live a holy life, being submitted to a local pastor, and so forth. If these basics are absent from your life, there is no way you are ready for a greater anointing of the Spirit.

The word "established" in Greek is the word *babaios* (ba-bai-os), which literally means "to make firm, steadfast, or settled." It describes something that is immovable and set in concrete.

Paul's intention is clear. He means to say, "If you want to be used in the greater anointings of God, then develop these firm, steadfast, immovable, settled traits in your life. Become established!"

Saints, God will not use us until we decide to be used. We can hang around the church, listening to the pastor preach and teach, and walk right out the door and decide to forget what he said during the service.

Or, we can say, "I'm here for the fight! I'm going to strip off this attitude. I'm going to take it all off!" And if we make this decision, then we are in a position to receive the first anointing of oil.

So many people come into the church and then leave, saying, "Well, I didn't get anything out of that message today." What was their attitude when they came to church? Did they strip themselves when they walked through that door? Were they there to be worked over? That is exactly what Paul means: First things first!

Paul says, "Now he which stablished us with you in Christ. . . ." Then, after this talk of being "established," he mentions the anointing, saying, ". . .and hath anointed us, is God."

The truth is, if you establish yourself in the local church, submit to a local pastor, allow him to teach, train, prepare, and instruct you — if you allow him to press the Word and the first application of the Spirit's oil hard and deep into your life — God will begin to take you to the next phase of your spiritual experience: THE GREATER ANOINTING.

Please understand, your commitment to the church, like an athlete's commitment and need for the *Palastra,* is not an option. It is an absolute requirement! This dedication and commitment will cause the Spirit of God to issue you another invitation: an invitation to come down the hall into the second anointing chamber, for the second, heavy-duty application of the Spirit's oil for your life.

## Oiled From Head to Toe With a Second Dose

Once the athlete had been coated with his first layer of oil, he was taken into a second room, called the *aleiplerion* (a-lei-ple-rion). In this room, he was dosed with a second, heavy application of anointing oil.

In fact, the trainer would take a vial of oil, turn it upside down, and pour the whole thing out until his entire body was completely covered with oil. This thick coat of oil remained on the athlete's body until the competition was completely over.

Some of the greatest Greek literature tells us that these athletes looked like they had been greased. *It was a thick coat of oil.* It would be as if someone took a great crock of cooking oil and rubbed it all over your body, from head to toe.

You ask, "Why would they take an athlete into a room and pour this oil all over him?"

Because this second, heavy application of oil made the athlete *slippery.* Therefore, when he entered into the fight, his adversary could not grab hold of him!

There's something else you need to know about this oil. Although there was a great storage room full of this oil in the *Palastra, the oil was not free.* The trainer had to pay for it out of his own pocketbook.

*The anointing oil was free to the athlete, but it was extremely expensive to the trainer.*

Trainers demanded high fees for their services, and a part of that fee was supposed to be used to purchase this expensive oil. The bulk of his high fee was used to purchase this needed oil.

This created a real problem: Because the athlete never had to think about buying the oil, or if he had enough money to buy *more* oil, he often *abused* it. Not realizing the great cost involved, athletes would carelessly wipe it off and then expect the trainer to come and pour another fresh dose all over him again.

## The Spirit's Oil Is Expensive

The Church, like the *Palastra,* has a great storage of oil; all the oil of the Spirit we'll ever need is stored away in the Church. Just like athletes of old, people now sit in the congregation and freely receive of the Word and the anointing, not realizing the great price the ministry had to pay to obtain it.

You see, *while it is free for believers who are training to do the work of ministry, this precious anointing is not free to those who are applying it.*

In a very real way, those who minister have paid for this anointing out of their own pocketbooks. However, it isn't purchased with cash or credit cards; it is obtained through dedication, seriousness, commitment, holiness, and hard work.

*Those who have come with a great ministry and a great anointing of the Spirit have lain before God and cried out for the anointing which you now so freely receive!*

Because the oil used in the *Palastra* was so expensive, one trainer alone was not able to provide all the oil that was necessary to anoint the athletes. The manager of the *Palastra,* also called the trainer (who is a type of the local pastor), did not have sufficient funds to purchase *all* the oil that was available for all the athletes. Therefore, the manager had to invite other trainers to help him purchase the anointing oil.

*This is a picture of the fivefold ministry.* The pastor is a wonderful gift, but the pastor cannot provide all of the Spirit's oil which you need. The apostle is wonderful and absolutely necessary, but he is just one person, and he cannot provide all the oil necessary, either. Although prophets seem to come splashing with all kinds of miraculous anointings, even they cannot provide all the oil needed. Neither can evangelists or teachers.

*There is no way one person or one gift can provide all the oil needed.* It simply is not possible. Therefore, God brings together a multitude of "trainers" — professional "oil-rubbers" — who come with the anointing of the Spirit that they have purchased out of their own lives, and they freely apply it to all the competitors; that is, the Church!

## Perfect Timing To Apply the Oil

There is something else important for you to understand about this second, heavy application of oil: It wasn't given out randomly, with no rhyme or reason.

Indeed, this heavy dose of oil was not in just any room of the *Palastra.* This second anointing chamber, the *aleiplerion,* was *temperature controlled!* The heavy anointing was withheld until the temperature was correct. When the temperature was perfectly controlled and correct, the oil would be applied.

This says to us that *there is a perfect, controlled temperature or right atmosphere, a place or a time in our lives, whereby the heavy anointing of God's Spirit comes upon us.* If you want to receive this heavy dose of the Spirit, you've got to get in *the right place* to receive it!

## The Real Exercise Begins

Once this second, heavy dose of oil was applied, *the real exercises and hardcore preparation began.*

The athletes were taken out into a small room, like a cubical. It was a small room with no roof, and sand covered its floor. This training room was designed to catch the heat of the sun, making it into a kind of sun-box or hot-box.

We are told by some historians that the temperatures in this room rose so high that the average man who had never endured such heat would have *died* if left there too long. It was in rooms like this that the athletes trained, fought, and prepared for the real fight!

You may be thinking, "Why in the world would they practice in such sweltering heat?"

Because the real competitions always took place during the hottest period of the year. And while many athletes were skilled, athletically fit, and had been through all kinds of grueling exercises, they were not able to endure the intense heat of the sun. With all their skill and training behind them, they still failed and were defeated *because the heat wore them out.*

That is often the problem with *head knowledge.* We study books, listen to tapes, watch videos, and see what other men have to say. But it's when we get out there in the heat of the conflict that we find out if we've really caught on!

*We need to be ready to take some heat!* I'm amazed by all these people who are constantly complaining about everything they've been through. The way we view life determines how we live life. If we walk around with a chip on our shoulder, with our feelings on our sleeve, we'll never survive a real conflict with the adversary. We'll be a pushover for him!

*We must never be afraid of the heat!* Yes, it's uncomfortable, and sometimes it's nearly unbearable. However, if we step out into the heat and say, "I'm going to learn to take it, fight in it, and win in the midst of it," we will be *the very best of combat zone fighters!*

## The Hotter the Conflict, the More Slippery the Oil

Keep in mind that this athlete was covered with a thick layer of oil! Although this horrible heat was difficult to endure, it really worked to the athlete's advantage. The hotter the conflict — the hotter this man became — the more slippery the oil on him became!

This is a wonderful thing about the Holy Spirit: When the devil turns up the heat, and the conflict becomes nearly unbearable, that heat makes you yield more to the anointing of the Spirit! And that anointing, if allowed to flow freely in the midst of a heated battle, will make you like *greased lightning!*

It won't matter how hard Satan tries to seize and catch you, because *you'll slip right out of his hands!* You'll suddenly become a target he can't catch! Thank God for this heavy dose of the Spirit's oil.

How would you like to be so anointed that even if the devil did *catch* you, he couldn't *keep* you? However, you can catch and keep him! Here's why.

The athletes of the early Greek world, although slippery with oil, would smack their hands down into the sand floor of this hot-box. Because their hands were already covered with oil, sand would stick to their palms, making them gritty, like sandpaper.

While their opponent could not hold them, they had no problem grabbing and holding their opponent! That oil, mixed with the sand, gave them ability to hold onto the enemy tightly, giving them *the edge* against their competitors!

*The Holy Spirit's anointing in our life always gives us the edge over the work of Satan!* Wouldn't you like to always have the upper hand over Satan? Wouldn't you enjoy always having the edge on him?

## Exercise Begins to the Tune of a Flute

Everyone did the same, exact exercises. While wrestlers practiced wrestling, they also practiced boxing. Boxers, in addition to boxing, also wrestled. In other words, if you were working out and training in the *Palastra,* you attempted to become fit in each of the combat sports: boxing, wrestling, and *pankration*.

*Perfection was their goal.* So committed were they to perfecting their art of athletic skills, they desired to have *rhythm* in their movements. Pay careful attention to this: Long-jumpers, discus throwers, boxers, wrestlers, and *pankratists* practiced and competed *to the accompaniment of the flute!*

Can you imagine attempting to throw the discus to the tune of the flute? How about boxing to the accompaniment of the flute? Can you see these *pankratists* kicking, biting, hitting, striking, breaking fingers, snapping backs, and so on, *to the accompaniment of the flute?*

These athletes were so committed to rhythm and beauty that when they competed, their movements and motions were dictated by the sound level and tempo of the instrument! If the flute played faster, they moved faster; if slower, they moved slower. If louder, they fought more boisterously. If lower, they were more low-key in their attacks.

Do you see how this applies to our lives spiritually? We need to be so fit, exercised, and spiritually prepared, that *we can fight and compete in the combat zone to the acompaniment of the Holy Spirit!*

Whatever tune He plays, that's what we need to do! When He tones it down, we need to tone it down. When He increases the volume, we need to increase our attacks against the adversary. We need to be tuned to the exact accompaniment of the Holy Spirit!

## Stronger and Tougher

Greek athletes did everything they could think of to become tougher. They exercised with weights, calisthenics, punching bags, shadow-boxing, kicking, gouging, and so forth. They wanted to become stronger and tougher!

Their weekly schedule consisted of several days of exhausting exercises, one day of rest, another day when they literally gorged themselves on food until it hurt, and then finally, one entire day — all day long — when they induced vomiting. This schedule applied to everyone, regardless of his physical condition. Even if you were sick, this was your schedule.

You may say, "Why?"

*Because they were committed to becoming hardened.* They wanted to be able to take *anything* their opponent dished out. Therefore, they made their daily lives difficult, so that when they were confronted by a real challenge, they could easily overcome it.

## Swallow Your Teeth If Necessary

So committed were Greek athletes to winning that, if wounded, they refused to allow their opponent to know it.

An early example of this fierce determination is the story of a boxer. He was hit extremely hard by his adversary, right in the middle of his mouth. The blow was so hard that it knocked many of his teeth out! However, rather than opening his mouth to spit out the broken teeth and blood, which would have alerted his opponent to his stricken condition, adding more fuel to the fire, *he chose to swallow the teeth!*

I think this is a wonderful example. When believers become whimpy and sit around constantly complaining, "My feelings are hurt!" Or, "Oh, the devil's out to get me!" Or, "I'm so wounded!" they are encouraging the devil to hit them again!

It's one thing to ask others to pray for you to be mended and healed, but it's quite another thing to sit around moaning and groaning because you've been hit! Why let the devil know he hit you with a hurtful blow? That's what faith is for! Stand up by faith, stand on the Word, grab hold of the Holy Spirit's powerful anointing — *and go after the devil again!*

*There is a place in God where you must decide to keep going, regardless of what has or will happen.* You must come to a place where you say, "I don't care how bad my feelings are hurt. I don't care how many times I've been stomped on! I'm not going to give the devil the satisfaction of knowing I've been wounded! Forget it: I'm going to get back up and fight!"

We must come to this place of fierce determination if we are genuinely serious combat zone fighters.

## A New Philosophy for the Church

If believers developed this type of philosophy, there would be a lot less *flesh* in the Church and a great deal more *victory!*

As it is, we still have local churches full of people who have never taken off their old clothes and gotten into a place of preparation. Yes, they come to church. They listen to the message. But so many have never really made a decision to enter into that first room to strip, bathe, and cleanse themselves, and be worked over by the Lord.

*Instead, the Church seems to be full of people who want shortcuts — people who somehow have convinced themselves that they are the exception to all these rules of preparation, exercise, hard training, and work.*

We need to pray for God to enable us to make the decision to strip off all obstacles, come into the *Palastra*, and be prepared by the Holy Spirit to fight!

## What To Do With Unused Oil

Once the athletic practice or competition was over, those who won or survived the games went back into that first room of the *Palastra*, where the hot, steamy baths were waiting for them.

Before stepping into those waters to cleanse and refresh themselves, they first scraped off all the unused oil still on their bodies, and poured it back into the oil vials to store it away until it was needed again.

This tells us the greatest anointings are given for struggle and combat. We don't need these great anointings to cook dinner or mow the lawn; we need the greatest anointings when there is a fight taking place!

Many immature people misunderstand the anointing of God. They think ministers — because they are so anointed in dynamic, public ministry — should constantly walk around in that same type of anointing. Thank God for the anointing, but the anointing is given when you need it, not so you can flaunt it and prove how spiritual you are!

When the battle is over and the conflict is won, the anointing normally subsides. This is so amazing to me personally. How odd it is to do great ministry for a solid week, see the sick healed, demons cast out, and the Word mightily poured into the lives of people. For the moment, it seems like this extra-special anointing will last forever. But when the meeting is over, and the demand is gone, that precious anointing subsides. . .*I didn't say it leaves!*

That anointing seems to lie dormant in the warrior's life until the heat of a new conflict arises, a new meeting begins, or Satan begins waging yet another battle. Then, miraculously, that anointing of the Spirit arises within the believer to do warfare again!

Thank God for this precious, *precious oil!*

## What About the Choir?

In Philippians 1:19, Paul says, "For I know that this shall turn to my salvation through your prayer, and the supply of the Spirit of Jesus Christ."

Especially notice that last phrase, ". . .the supply of the Spirit of Jesus Christ." The word "supply" is extremely significant to this issue of the Spirit's anointing, for it tells us how much anointing of the Spirit is available to us right now — *at this very moment.*

The word "supply" is from the very old Greek word *epichoregias* (epi-cho-re-gi-as). What an odd word this is! Literally translated, it means "on behalf of the choir"!

What does a choir have to do with the anointing of the Holy Spirit? Why does Paul use such an odd word to describe the Spirit's provision in our lives?

This word *epichoregias* ("supply") has a history that is wonderful! It is the story of a choir that went broke...

After many months of preparation and training, just when it was about time to stage a large musical presentation for the public, the choir, actors, and orchestra ran out of money. For all intents and purposes, this meant their show was over, and all their labor, tears, work, and commitment seemed to have been for nothing.

Then a very wealthy citizen from the area heard about their plight. Because they had worked so hard, he couldn't stand the thought of all their labor being wasted. Therefore, he came to them and gave a financial contribution "for the choir."

This contribution was so massive, it overwhelmed them. In fact, it was far too much money! They didn't need this vast sum, and they didn't know what to do with it all. It was an incredible contribution made "for the choir."

So this Greek word *epichoregias* ("supply") comes from this story. By using this word, Paul plainly tells us, "When you have done all you can do — you've trained, worked, prepared, and done your part — then God comes in to make a contribution on your behalf!

"He gives you an enormous 'supply' of the Spirit! There is so much Spirit available to you, you'll never know how to use it all. If you tried to use it up, you would find it was impossible! *God has made a wonderful, huge contribution of the Spirit's anointing into your life!"*

## If You Like Prizes...

In Second Timothy 2:5, Paul has been telling Timothy to get ready for a fight. By using athletic terms, he makes his message clear and simple: Paul is telling Timothy to quit sitting around feeling sorry for himself and letting the devil know he has hit him hard.

Paul's advice is, "Get up and get to work preparing and training. You've still got a job to do and a devil to fight!" Paul states in this verse, "And if a man also strive for masteries, yet is he not crowned, except he strive lawfully."

We've already covered the phrases "strive for masteries" and "strive lawfully." However, there is one extremely important part of this verse still untouched by this study: the phrase "yet is he not crowned...."

The word "crowned" is extremely important, just like all the other phrases we've covered, because it conveys yet another vivid image to Timothy (and to us)!

The Greek word for "crowned" is the work *stephanos* (ste-pha-nos), which in other places is translated "diadem, royal crown, or crown of glory." There is no room for wondering what Paul's statement about this crown implies!

Paul is continuing the idea of athletic events. However, now he moves beyond the rules, practices, oil, *Palastra,* trainers and equippers, and he begins talking about *the rewards given to the best athletes.*

Those who finished first at the games received a beautiful crown made out of laurel leaves. It is *this crown* which Paul now refers to.

When you understand the connotations carried with this crown — *this reward* — then you know why the athletes were willing to pay such a high price to compete.

Oh, would to God that we, too, would understand the magnificent rewards that Jesus Christ has waiting for us! In Revelation 22:12, the Lord Jesus says, "And, behold, I come quickly; and *my reward is with me....*"

Paul never lost sight of his reward for service. Remember, he said, "Henceforth there is laid up for me *a crown of righteousness,* which the Lord, the righteous judge, shall give me at that day. . ." (2 Timothy 4:8).

In Second Corinthians 5:10, Paul tells us, "For we must all appear before the judgment seat of Christ; that every one *may receive* the things done in his body, according to that he hath done, whether it be good or bad."

Often we become so involved in the training, preparation, and heat of the conflict that the conflict is all we can see. *Unfortunately, we become nearsighted and forgetful.*

We get so involved with our current conflict and fight of faith that we cease to see beyond the fight to *the reward* awaiting us because we were faithful to the end! Or, we become so consumed with the conflict that it is all we can see or think about, and we forget that Jesus Christ is waiting and has *His reward* in His hand.

## The Crown of Victory

This "crown of glory," "diadem," or "victor's crown" was reserved for the winner of a competition. Now Paul uses this analogy to describe what God has waiting for those who fight a good fight of faith.

If you won an athletic victory in classical Greece, the ancients placed a laurel crown upon your head. Although the crown was not worth much, being made out of nothing more than laurel leaves, nuts, sometimes apples, or pine cones, and twine, it represented something very important. It was *symbolic* of a promise.

Today we would simply give the winner a large check representing a huge cash gift. But in those days, there were no checkbooks. Therefore, in this huge ceremonial celebration where many people gathered to watch the victor be awarded, they would give him a crown, and this crown represented *monetary rewards.*

Not only money was given the victor, but other material possessions as well: homes, servants, and other luxuries were piled upon those who won the athletic contests. So great were these rewards that the entire ancient world knew about them. They were *incredible, unbelievable rewards!*

This, of course, explains why athletes were willing to undergo such adverse training and discipline. It wasn't just for the sake of discipline and endurance; it was because they wanted that huge monetary reward. *They were after the cash!*

There's still more! In addition to all the material rewards, frequently the greatest winners were nearly deified. Monuments, statues, and huge memorials were built to commemorate their victories. Many of these statues still stand to this very day — living memorials of their accomplishments.

## What Does All This Mean to You?

Like Timothy, you probably have had to deal with some type of adversity in your life. In fact, you may be there *right now*. Would you like to see your situation changed? Would you like to see this continuing conflict end?

Then Second Timothy 2:5 is just for you! Paul says, "And if a man also strive for masteries, yet is he not crowned, except he strive lawfully."

If you determine that you are going for the prize; that you are not an amateur, but, rather, a professional; if you're willing to strip all the extra, unneeded baggage from your life; then you'll see your circumstances turn around! You'll end up the winner — *and you'll receive the victor's crown!*

And like the athletes of old, if you truly take a difficult stand — even in the midst of adverse circumstances — and you continue to stand in faith anyway — your fight will be remembered for ages to come!

Think of all the great men and women of God from the past whom we still remember, read about, and attempt to imitate. Their stand, their conflict, their fight, their fierce determination to win the fight, has forever placed them in our hearts to be remembered.

It is because they fought so well that we remember people like Paul, Timothy, Luke, John, and also many giants of the faith in recent centuries. Consider *Charles Wesley, Charles G. Finney, Billy Sunday, Charles F. Parham, Maria Woodworth-Etter, Smith Wigglesworth, William Branham, John G. Lake, or Kathryn Kuhlman.* All of them are remembered — not for their great educations, but for their *accomplishments by faith!*

As Hebrews 11:32-39 says,

> **And what shall I more say? for the time would fail me to tell of Gedeon,** [Gideon] **and of Barak, and of Samson, and of Jephthae; of David also, and Samuel, and of the prophets:**
>
> **Who through faith subdued kingdoms, wrought righteousness, obtained promises, stopped the mouths of lions,**
>
> **Quenched the violence of fire, escaped the edge of the sword, out of weakness were made strong, waxed valiant in fight, turned to flight the armies of the aliens.**
>
> **Women received their dead raised to life again: and others were tortured, not accepting deliverance; that they might obtain a better resurrection:**
>
> **And others had trial of cruel mockings and scourgings, yea, moreover of bonds and imprisonment:**
>
> **They were stoned, they were sawn asunder, were tempted, were slain with the sword: they wandered about in sheepskins and goatskins; being destitute, afflicted, tormented;**
>
> **(Of whom the world was not worthy:) they wandered in deserts, and in mountains, and in dens and caves of the earth.**
>
> **And these all, having obtained a good report through faith. . . .**

These faithful ones, because they "obtained a good report through faith," are with us and in our minds *forever. Your strong, consistent, determined faith will put you on the map!*

In the same way, God has called you to "endure hardness as a good soldier of Jesus Christ," He has also called you to "strive for masteries" in order that you will be rewarded both now and in the life to come!

This was the message Timothy needed to be reminded of. *You need to be reminded of it, too.*

In the next verse, Paul moves on to his third illustration for Timothy, who was still in the heat of the battle. Paul says, "The husbandman that laboureth must be first partaker of the fruits" (Second Timothy 2:6).

In the next chapter, we will see why Paul now compared Timothy and us with hard-working farmers. In this verse, God is making us an absolutely fabulous promise!

## Chapter 8
# Reaping the Benefits of the Combat Zone

Paul switches illustrations once again to make another very important point about life in the combat zone.

Suddenly, the strenuous athletic talk stops, and he moves to pick up another illustration of how we should view our life in the combat zone. He begins teaching about *a hard-working farmer!*

This must have left Timothy's mind whirling! Paul has already told him to endure and fight like *a soldier,* then to prepare and train like *an athlete.* And now he tells Timothy to work hard like a *farmer!*

It's almost as thought Paul says, "Timothy, you need to be a good soldier of Jesus Christ! No, as good as that example is, it's not good enough. *I know,* you need to train and prepare like an athlete does. Son, you need to have the determination and commitment of an athlete.

"Oh, forget the athletic example, too! It's good, but not complete enough to convey what I mean. What I really mean to say is, you need to be hard working, like a farmer!

"I know what I mean: Timothy, *you need to be all three of these things! You must fight like a soldier, train like an athlete, and be committed to work, work, and work like a farmer! You must view yourself as a soldier, an athlete, and a farmer."*

## A Hard-Working Farmer

In Second Timothy 2:6, Paul continues his message by stating, "The husbandman that laboureth must be first partaker of the fruits."

In this verse, there are four very important messages. Notice the words "husbandman" and "laboureth" and the phrases "must be" and "first partaker of the fruits."

Paul is conveying pictures of farming life. As you read on, you will see how these four pictures relate to those of us who are living in the combat zone.

In the first place, Paul mentions the "husbandman." The word "husbandman" in Greek refers to "one who tills or works the soil." It would be accurate to translate it as a "soil-worker, or a soil-tiller."

The Greek word for a husbandman is an often-used word, and there is no doubt that Paul is referring to the activities of *a farmer.* And, more than this, he is referring to a *hard-working* farmer. Notice how he continues: "the husbandman *that laboureth....*"

The word "labour" in Greek is the word *kopos* (ko-pos). The word *kopos* doesn't refer just to regular work, but rather *to the hardest type of work.* We would say this was a man working to the point of "sweat and tears."

By using the word *kopos,* Paul is painting us a picture of a farmer working in the heat of the afternoon sun, during the hottest period of the year. The ground as hard as clay, there is little moisture, and the work is *strenuous.*

The farmer is *plowing and sowing.* Then, after he has finished working one row of his garden, he turns at the end of the row and starts all over again on the next row — *plowing and sowing!*

By the end of the day, he is physically exhausted, mentally drained, drenched with perspiration, and covered with dirt. He has done a hard day's work!

By using this illustration, Paul is telling us once again that living in the combat zone can be hard, difficult, and exhausting. However, rather than complain and moan about it, we might as well face the facts: *Someone has to get out there and do the job!*

If a farmer wants to reap the benefits of a crop, that means he's got to plow and plant. The unbearable heat doesn't change the necessity of the task. Regardless, his job is to plow and plant.

And if we do our job in the combat zone faithfully, like a hard-working farmer, *we will reap the benefits of our crop.* As Paul said, "The husbandman that laboureth must be *first partaker of the fruits.*" The fruits belong to the hard worker first. Everyone else eats after him!

## Farming in the Middle East

The tradition of farming in the Middle East reaches back for thousands of years.

The farming activities of the first century are well documented. At least fifty Greek authors contributed written material on the subject of farming. Unfortunately, these writings of the Greeks on the subject rarely survived.

However, the records of the Romans are still abundant today. Varro, the wonderful scholar, farmer, politician, and soldier who lived in the century preceding the birth of the Lord Jesus Christ, wrote *tremendous details* about the life of a farmer.

Columella, a writer who wrote about ten years after the crucifixion of Jesus, also recorded many activities of first century farming. And Pliny, the famous writer from the first century who wrote about many subjects, wrote substantial material that was given almost entirely to the study of country life, farming, and husbandry.

History bears out the fact that in countries where Christianity flourished, there was a highly organized system of farming. The areas surrounding Israel were agricultural areas. It was for this reason that Jesus often used farming examples in His parables. These were examples taken directly from the lifestyle that affected the majority of the people during His time.

In fact, most writers agree that until recent years, the historic methods of farming in Israel and the surrounding Mediterranean areas changed very little from thousands of years ago! This means that the same methods of plowing, sowing, and harvesting that were in use during the time of the Lord Jesus were still used until recent years.

Therefore, it is easy for us to obtain an accurate picture of what Paul meant when he compared us with a hard-working, Middle Eastern farmer of the first century.

## The Job of Sowing Seed

The farming which Paul spoke of was not done with highly developed machinery. Rather, it was nearly all done *by hand, individually.* The reaping was done *by hand* as well. This is an important point when you consider that Jesus likens the teaching and preaching of the Word to the work of a farmer.

In Matthew 13, Jesus spoke two parables in which He uses the illustration of *a farmer* (or "sower") to describe the preaching of the Word. In both parables, you find the farmer is *personally involved* in the sowing of seed and the reaping of the fruit.

Concerning teaching, preaching, and sowing the Word into the heart — like a farmer would sow seed into a field — the Lord said, "Behold *a sower* went forth to sow; And when *he sowed*. . ." (Matthew 13:3,4). Jesus spoke again in the same manner in verse 24: "The kingdom of heaven is likened unto *a man* which sowed good seed in *his* field. . . ."

Notice in both of these examples the sower himself — *personally* — goes into the field to sow the seed. Also notice the personal, individual touch in Jesus' words. He doesn't say "many sowers went forth." Instead, He says *"a sower. . . ."*

This is in perfect agreement with the historic records we have of farming methods of that day.

The farmer was *personally involved* in all the activities of the field. It was his farm; therefore, it was *his* responsibility. This farm was so precious to him that it required his complete, total attention.

There is another important point here: *Sowing the seed into the field was done primarily by one individual.* Even though it was time consuming for one person to do the total work of sowing, this very important task was, nevertheless, done by *one person only — the farmer.* It was his job to sow, and no one else's.

Later, when harvest time came, many workers could come into the field to help reap the harvest. However, the planting of seed — because it was such a crucial, vital job — was the responsibility of the farmer himself.

You may ask, "Why is this important?"

Because it tells us we must become *personally involved* in the work God has called us to do. And, because we have been given a trust over God's field, the Church, we cannot depend on someone else to do our job for us. Neither can we simply bring in "hired hands" to help because we are exhausted or tired of the occupation. Our ministry is important, and *we must give it our own personal touch.*

## Maintaining a Personal Touch

We live in a day when Christianity has become computerized, highly mechanical, and mass produced, so to speak. Thank God for all these technological advances. Because of them, the Gospel is being spread to every area of the world. We use many of these methods in our own ministry. But we must never forget that the Gospel needs *a personal touch.*

With all of our God-given technological advances, it seems the Gospel has lost much of its personal touch. It is so easy to reach people through television, radio, satellites, computerized telephone messages, the mail, and so on, that we have come to neglect the warm, intimate, caring ministry that should *always* accompany the Gospel ministry.

These modern ways of reaching people are easy and non-threatening, for the most part. If you've ever done door-to-door evangelism, then you know the feeling one gets when a door is slammed in your face for attempting to share the Gospel.

It is far easier to simply put out a mass mail-out. That way, no doors are slammed in your face. If the people don't like what you have to say, they can just throw your letter away.

A computerized telephone message doesn't care if the listener listens or hangs up. It has neither feelings nor emotions. As one evangelist said, "It's great trying to reach people with this new computerized telephone device! You never get rejected, never get cussed out, and never have to answer any difficult Bible questions! Really, there's no personal involvement, and it doesn't require any of your personal time. You just let the telephone do all the work!"

Please don't misunderstand me: I'm thrilled for all the thousands of people who are being reached via these different methods. I'm thrilled with *any* method that brings people to Jesus Christ. However, we must never allow these advanced methods to replace the personal touch of "the sower." For the most part, sowing should be done *by hand!*

There is still *no replacement* for the personal touch of a caring *pastor;* the powerful, personal influence of an *apostle;* the soul-stirring message and presence of a *prophet;* the personal, fine-tuned anointing of an excellent *teacher;* the strong, fiery presence of an *evangelist;* and the impact of warm-hearted *believers* on a lost soul.

Even though our ministry grows and our outreaches expand, we who are sowers of the Word must make every effort to be personally involved with the field.

## How Does This Apply to the Combat Zone?

When warfare is all around, and the battle is getting more heated, it would be easy to back up, protect yourself, and let someone or something else do all the work for you.

When rejection has hit you on many different occasions, the temptation for you would be to simply send everyone a taped message or a mass letter. This way, their response can't hurt you again! *I've* done this; *you've* done this; and I think nearly *everyone* has done this.

You see, Satan wants to keep us out of the field! He wants to keep you and the anointing of God away from the saints.

It is true that the anointing can be transmitted through taped cassette or video messages, letters, radio and television programs, and even through prayer cloths.

*But there is no substitute for the anointing that is passed on through one's personal presence!* God meant for the anointing to be passed on through your life!

Regardless of the spiritual climate, or the difficulty of the hour, we must be directly, personally involved when it comes to placing the Gospel seed into the hearts of men.

Like a farmer who works the field in the hottest period of the day, during the hottest time of the year, during sweltering heat and in hardened soil, we must not neglect our place. Even if the job is hard, we must do it. If we do not give it our all, the job will not get done. Therefore, our place is to be in the field.

## Two Primary Methods of Sowing Seed

There were primarily two methods used to sow seed at the time of Jesus.

First, the ground was *prepared, plowed,* and *made ready* to receive the seed. Once the ground was properly prepared, the seed was scattered and then plowed into the ground by the farmer.

Or, second, the seed was scattered over hard, *unprepared soil*. Later, it was plowed under as the farmer worked over it with his oxen.

Of the two methods, the first was better. The first method is a picture of sowing the Word *inside* the Church. Inside the Church we have opportunity to work the soil, prepare the believers' hearts, and get them ready to receive God's Word. Then, after receiving the seed, it can be worked further and deeper into their hearts by constant teaching.

Most farmers simply scattered the seed into prepared soil at random. This was fine, but there was still another method which was better than this.

*The best farmers would actually sit down in the dirt of the field to personally plant the seed into the soil by hand, one by one — one plant at a time.*

By doing this, not only did they make certain the seed was safely planted; they also were able to keep the rows in an *orderly* fashion.

This tells us that careful sowing is better than simply scattering the seed. While both methods are fine, the second allows you to plant in an orderly fashion. This, of course, helps the reaper when it comes time to harvest the fruit of the field. *The more orderly the field, the easier the harvest!*

This, of course, is a picture of ministry. To scatter the seed on prepared soil is representative of sowing God's Word into the prepared heart of a church or a *congregation*. The church is *always* good soil.

Notice again the two ways to do this: scatter it randomly, or sit down to personally plant it into the soil by hand, in a very organized, orderly fashion.

Preaching the Word to a congregation or a large crowd of people is like scattering seed *randomly* on good soil. It is quite a challenge to preach or teach to a group like this. In fact, the bigger the field, the bigger the challenge to touch all of the field with seed. Why?

Because in any one group, you always have a multiplicity of problems and backgrounds represented. Therefore, it isn't always possible to zero in on one specific subject. One message must touch the issue of strongholds, marriage difficulties, personal problems, finances, and so forth. This is a manner in which every pastor must plant. However, there is an even more effective way to plant the seed of God's Word.

What is it? To personally sit down in the dirt, the soil — which is the Church and her members — and to plant the seed by hand in an organized, orderly fashion. This is what *discipleship* is all about: personally planting the seed, covering it with protection, watering it, and pouring fertilizer on it in order to ensure its growth.

There is another important consideration! When you sow the Word from the pulpit, although you are attempting to scatter the seed into as many people as possible during that service, *try to put some organization into it.*

A message from God that is organized, has continuity, flows with a previous message, and links with a series of messages to follow, helps keep the rows of plants (the people!) in line.

On the other hand, *disjointed messages* — a message here, a message there and — BOOM! — another new subject again, is often confusing to the saints. They need help to keep their spiritual lives in order. Many of them do not have the capacity to organize their spiritual thoughts. Yet *they desire order and organization.* Therefore, we must help them!

Again, the more orderly the field, the easier the harvest. We must make the harvest as easy as possible in order to help the saints grow.

## Sowing on Hardened Soil

The other type of sowing (scattering seed upon hardened soil) is representative of sowing on the *outside* of the Church (in the world), or in a *backslidden* church.

This would represent the act of preaching to the lost, or sending the Word into a hardened society that is unprepared and not right with God. Because their hearts are not ready to receive seed, this is a most difficult method of sowing spiritual seed. It must be plowed, plowed, and plowed deeply into the dirt afterwards, or it will not take root. This is especially difficult if the spiritual soil is hardened.

When I think of those who have given their lives to reach pagan countries, or those who are endeavoring to reach large, difficult cities like New York City, I can't help but think of a farmer working on *hardened soil.* We must pray for those on the front lines, where the soil is totally unprepared to receive spiritual seed and where there is little sensitivity to the things of God.

This is the hardest type of seed-sowing.

While this second method of sowing would mainly be used in evangelistic-type ministry, it is also a method of sowing within the Church from time to time. When a church family is spiritually brain-dead, backslidden, and neutral, it can be quite difficult to sow seed into them.

Thank God for pastors who have helped prepare the hearts of their people. A prepared heart or congregation is a joy to teach! They soak up every word they hear!

On the other hand, preaching to a congregation which has no appreciation for the Word and no desire for more of God is an extremely hard challenge. In such cases, you must ignore their lack of response, preach regardless of what their reaction may be, and then dig, dig, dig, and dig — plow, plow, plow, and plow — until you get that seed down on the inside of them. This type of ministry is not fun!

Fun or not, it must be done. This is why God calls Timothy (and us) a "husbandman," or a "farmer." Our function as ministry gifts is to get that seed into the field! This is why Paul calls us the "husbandman that *laboureth* . . . ." At times this is *real labor!*

## Keep Your Eye on the Weather, Bugs, and Birds

The time of sowing seed was extremely important to the farmer. The newly planted seed could be easily affected by weather, bugs, and birds. These devouring birds were referred to by Jesus in the parable of the Sower and the Seed in Matthew 13. He calls them the "fowls of the air": *demonic devourers* sent forth to gobble the Word out of the human heart.

The serious, responsible farmer was always careful to watch as the young crops grew and matured. It is noted that the *early spring winds could be vicious.* This, of course, was a danger to the soil and seed as well. A strong wind storm could turn the soil, thus carrying away the precious seed.

It is interesting to note that *the most violent weather of the year always coincided with the perfect time to plant seed.* In the spirit realm, this is true as well.

When the time is right — you have a grand, new open door to reach people, and you know you must take advantage of this golden moment provided by God — strong winds are nearly always blowing. They accompany the planting of the Word!

However, we must not be afraid of the vicious winds of opposition. Neither can we wait until later, when the winds have ceased, to plant the seed. If we wait, we *lose* our opportunity. Therefore, we must seize the opportunity, pray over our seed, protect the work of God, and get into that field. We *cannot* allow the winds to dictate our obedience.

This must have been exactly what Timothy thought was occurring to his own field, his local church in Ephesus. After several years of good growth, an unbelievable demonic storm had arisen with a vengeance against the Early Church.

Nero's persecution of the saints was creating the worst catastrophe in the history of the young Church. Many believers were being swept away by the vicious winds of fear, and many others were being swept away by death itself.

Timothy could not back up, like others had done, to wait for the storm to blow over. His task was to be in the field. The fact that this satanic opposition was coming against him was the greatest indicator that he was *in the right place at the right time* to plant seed!

In light of all these possible attacks, a good farmer would stay close to the field to assure its safety; especially if his crop was still young and immature. If foul weather, hail storms, birds, locusts, or other insects attacked, his job was to be in that field doing everything within his power to protect the tender plants from destruction.

Likewise, one who sows God's Word must keep his eye on the crop (God's growing, maturing Church), especially when the plants are young and are just beginning to take root. This is when the enemy will attempt to attack, destroy, and devour the seed of God's Word so recently planted in their hearts.

## Winds of Opposition

Although we do not have a Nero to deal with today, we do have winds of opposition: *foul weather!* Strange teachings, error, seducing spirits, rebellion, betrayers, sabotage — all of these vicious winds have the power to turn the soil of a young believer's heart, thus carrying away the seed that was planted within him or her.

In the same manner, a young church, or even a church that is old, but just recently is experiencing a new vitalization by God's Spirit, can be adversely affected by these winds of satanic attack.

Satan has a way of causing a disgusting situation that offends, or ruins an individual's faith by causing a notable leader to fall. These strong, vicious winds seem to always carry some precious seed away, thus destroying the faith of some.

Many ministries today are experiencing "foul weather" in the area of *finances*. The winds of opposition are trying to drive the "sowers" out of the field. We absolutely, emphatically cannot allow these winds to control us. What a strategy Satan has! Drive the sower out of the field, and then his harvest will never come in!

If we allow these winds to dictate to us, we will be driven back into protectionism, defeat, and ruin. If we rationalize, "Maybe we should sit back and wait a while," it will simply delay the harvest. There will never be a harvest if we do not do our job. *Therefore, we must defy the odds, come against the foul weather of the spirit realm, and get back into the field!*

The situation will be no better later. Even if you do sit back to relax, rest, and wait, when you start planting seed again, the winds will come right back! We must learn to live with the wind and do our job of sowing, even if it looks like we must do it in the face of a *tornado!*

The fact that the winds are blowing strong means you are doing your job right, and you are doing it at the correct moment! *Foul weather nearly always accompanies the planting of seed.*

## Soaking the Seed With Protection

By the time of the New Testament, chemicals had already been introduced to protect the seed from insects. Primitive as these chemicals were, they worked.

Before the seed was sown, it was first soaked in a powerful liquid solution. The solution didn't hurt the seed, but it was deadly to the vile insects that would attempt to eat the seed once placed in the soil.

*Soaking the seed is crucial!*

In the same way they covered their seed with a chemical solution, we must cover the seed of God's Word with prayer and the blood of Jesus Christ.

If we thoroughly saturate our ministry, prophetic message, preaching, teaching, and instruction with prayer

— *before we preach or teach it* — less spiritual seed will be devoured by the enemy.

Often we become so busy preparing, we neglect the important, vital task of saturating the Word with prayer. Our prayers act as *protection!*

If the Word is covered and soaked in prayer, we will see more fruitfulness and more spiritual rooting take place in the flock. If Satan cannot blow the seed away, he will attempt to send in *"creepy crawlers"* to eat it right in the soil.

This is an especially damaging attack! Why? Because once the seed is in the soil, or is sown into the heart, you can no longer see it. In fact, you won't know that it has been eaten or destroyed until it is too late.

When it's time for the seed to produce, and no growth takes place, that's when you realize the seed was eaten or devoured by insects *from within!*

These "insects" may be bad attitudes, inward sin, demonic attack, and so forth. What eats the seed *isn't* important. Then, what *is* important? That we soak the seed with protection so it *cannot* be eaten!

With all the destruction taking place in Timothy's church, it makes one wonder if he had saturated the Word he was sowing in prayer. Perhaps Timothy, like many of us, faithfully prepared to deliver God's Word, but forgot to pray and soak the seed with protection! *This omission can be fatal to the seed!*

## Has the Enemy Attacked Your Personal Field?

What if this is a description of you? Has your life, business, ministry, or church been attacked by demonic fowls and insects? Have you been sowing, sowing, and sowing with *no results?*

I meet many pastors who are experiencing spiritual attacks in their churches. It is too late for some of them to save the crop. Satan's work of infestation has already taken over their church and, really, it is now beyond their control.

If this is you, you must remember there are plenty of new seasons still ahead of you! Every farmer occasionally experiences crop failure. But he doesn't stop farming because of one bad year! He has too much invested in his farm to give up that easily. He's put years of work into that farm, invested lots of money into his machinery, and has given his life to his profession. Just because one crop failed doesn't mean the next one will fail, too!

Likewise, you have too much invested in your ministry to give up now! You have put years of work and time into your calling! You have planted all your finances in it, and you have too much spiritual machinery to stop planting now! Just because one crop failed doesn't mean you're finished! When God speaks to your heart and you know it is time to start planting again, go for it!

Fear may try to control you and keep you from trying again. However, you must think of yourself like a farmer. A farmer doesn't stop farming because he's had one or even several bad years of farming. He keeps planting that seed in hopes of a bumper crop. *One good, bumper crop can make up for all those bad years of failure!*

Pick up your bag of seed and start planting the Word in lives again. *If you recognize you made mistakes in the past, then make the changes you must make to be a better farmer the next time around.*

Soak that precious seed in prayer and the blood before you plant it this time. Protect it, watch over it, and wait for your crop to come in. The next spiritual season may be a bumper crop year!

## Harvest Time Finally Arrives

Psalm 126:5 says, "They that sow in tears shall reap in joy." Ecclesiastes 3:2 says there is "a time to sow, and a time to reap that which has been sown." Eventually, the time to reap the benefits arrives!

*Pay attention to this important note: The time of harvesting in Bible days depended entirely upon the climate in your specific area.*

Even today, altitudes and temperatures vary tremendously in Israel, so harvest time comes at different times for different areas. In one low-lying district, harvest time may be in full swing while districts in higher altitudes will still be weeks, or even a full month, from their harvest.

*Temperature, altitude, and climate* determine the harvest time for each area.

Rarely do all areas harvest simultaneously. And this is good news! If every area had to be harvested simultaneously, there wouldn't be enough workers to bring the harvest into the barn! It would put a strain on the entire community, and much of the harvest would be missed — left to rot in the fields.

Because the harvesting varies from area to area, it permits the workers to work one area after another. This allows them space and time to develop in the art of reaping. Because of these varied periods of the harvest, it gives place to the finest reapers — reapers who have much opportunity to practice their skill — and almost none of the harvest is lost.

## Should We Be Jealous of Another's Success?

Often, ministries, churches, pastors, and even church members feel left out, hurt, or upset when they hear of a neighboring, similarly believing church or ministry that is experiencing growth.

If you have been working at your ministry a long time and have pure motives, it may be confusing to you to have to deal with someone else's success. It almost makes you look at yourself and ask, "What's wrong with me? Why am I not experiencing that kind of growth? God, am I where I'm supposed to be? Am I out of your perfect will?"

There is nothing wrong with asking those kinds of questions. It's always good to take a look at yourself and ask questions. It's good to ask, inspect, and see if you are hindering a move of God, or if you need to make changes in your personal life and style of ministry that will speed up a harvest.

However, you must not forget that the harvest time depends on several things: *temperature, climate, and altitude.*

Perhaps you live in a city where the temperature isn't right yet for a large harvest. Perhaps the spiritual climate is still getting ready for a move of God's Spirit. It may simply be that the other church or ministry reached harvest time a little before you.

This doesn't necessarily mean you've missed out! It tells you that your climate is not ready just yet to yield a harvest — *but harvest time will come!*

You can see this change of climate and harvesting in how God touches nations, or even states and cities. Right now there is a major harvest occurring in the Orient; especially in Korea and the Philippines. It seems there is also a major move now on the continent of Africa. These are areas where the climate is right for reaping. The *emphasis* has moved into a new field.

This same type of change can be seen in the different states of a nation. For a while, a major move of God will seem to consolidate in one area of the nation. Then it will seem to subside and *the emphasis will move to another area* whose harvest time has come. Then, after touching that field and bringing in the harvest, God will move the emphasis of reaping again.

Does this mean God is finished with the other areas, or is simply leaving some vicinities out altogether? No, *each according to its own temperature, climate, and altitude will come into a period of reaping and harvesting.*

This applies to your church and your ministry, too.

## Who Does the Reaping?

While the farmer was personally responsible to sow the seed into the soil, it was *impossible* for him to bring in the harvest single-handedly. Therefore, many workers were employed to help bring in the harvest.

When the harvest was just beginning to come in, the farmer and his immediate family did the reaping. This early harvest was small and easy to handle by the farmer and his family. They took great joy in reaping the first fruit; this is what they had been working for! This was their way of enjoying the first fruits and inspecting the harvest to see how good it was.

If it looked like a bumper-crop year, the smart farmer had already trained and prepared other workers. When the farmer could no longer handle the massive reaping and harvesting alone, he would send word to these other trained reapers, who would come to assist him in the joy of reaping.

Again, this is a picture of the Church: While the pastor can handle a small, early harvest — and wants to pick the first fruit — it isn't possible for him to handle a massive harvest by himself. Therefore, like a smart farmer, he must train and prepare the saints, "equipping them to do the work of the ministry" (Ephesians 4:12).

If *willing* believers are trained and prepared before the harvest comes, then reaping and harvesting will be a joy! However, if God sends a large harvest, and there are no trained workers, a large harvest can be *a curse!* Most of the harvest will never be taken advantage of and will lay rotting in the field.

Unfortunately, this has happened many times. Large, God-sent harvests have rotted in the fields because of a lack of preparation. I've heard it over and over again: "We just didn't realize so many people would respond. We weren't ready for this kind of response. We simply were not prepared."

After praying years for a large spiritual bumper crop, finally it arrives — and is missed, left in the field to rot, because no one trained and prepared in advance to bring the harvest into the barn, the Church.

What a shame! To finally have the blessing of God on your church, community, or ministry, and then miss your opportunity to reap!

Let us be careful not to make this mistake. We must do our vital work of preparation before the harvest time arrives!

## How To Get Rid of Locusts

Another significant danger to the farmer and his field was the threat of *devouring locusts.*

Locusts were a farmer's most horrid worry and cause for concern and fear. They were the worst nightmare possible. Just one large swarm of locusts could ravage an entire field in a matter of days, or sometimes in a matter of *hours.*

To make matters worse, farmers in Bible days did not have any sophisticated machinery or pesticides to remove these horrible scavengers from the plants in their fields.

And because the locusts were so numerous, it was *impossible* to remove them by hand. There weren't enough workers in the entire land to combat the thousands upon thousands (if not millions) of locusts that could light upon one man's field. Also, locusts eat so fast that the field would be destroyed before any work had begun.

*Locusts didn't make their grand appearance until the crop was grown and it was time for harvest!*

Why? Because that is when there was something to eat and chew! Prior to this, there was nothing of consequence for them to devour. Therefore, they waited until the seed had grown, the crop was beautiful and nearly matured — just about ready to be reaped — and then they would come to eat up everything in their path.

*The locusts came to devour the fields at harvest time!*

At first, it seemed there was no remedy for this situation. If your field was infested with locusts, you simply lost your harvest. The farmers knew of no plan or mechanism to remove these destroyers. They didn't have any pesticides. Then, finally, they came up with a last-ditch effort — a counterattack against these vile creatures.

*They discovered locusts hate smoke!*

Rather than letting the locusts eat the field, they learned to start a big fire. The size of the locust infestation determined how large a fire they would kindle. If the infestation was large, they would pile heaps and heaps of wood onto the fire to create a massive blaze and dense, dense smoke. If the locust attack was smaller, it required a smaller fire and less smoke.

With a huge fire burning, the smoke from the blaze poured upward into the sky, billowing gray and black smoke until the air was filled with ash and pollution.

When the smoke *densely* filled the air, their counterattack worked! The locusts, unable to breathe, would be suffocated to death. Eventually, they would fall out of the air, right into the burning fire, where they burned until completely consumed.

*Smoke gets rid of locusts.*

## Holy Ghost Smoke

In a similar fashion, we who sow God's Word into hearts must learn how to deal with "locusts," the demonic spirits or scavengers who come to eat up the harvest for which we've been waiting.

Just like the locusts of the air, demon spirits may allow the crop to grow for a while. They may wait to attack until the crop has begun to mature and you're headed for your harvest season. That is when they can do the most destruction!

Often, because we haven't had any previous attack, and things appear to be going along nicely, we forget the threat of spiritual attack. It is *then*, when we are neglectful of this possibility, that the enemy attacks.

He waits until the ministry is growing, maturing, and finally doing its best work. Then, like locusts descending on a field, he attacks, sending unbelievable hordes of opposition into our camp.

It is remarkable how a good church or ministry can blow up almost overnight! Hundreds of churches and ministries in recent years have been wiped off the map forever by a surprise attack from Satan's headquarters.

*We must not allow ourselves to become blind to the possibility of attack.* None of us is above this type of predicament. Regardless of how sweet things look, how green the pasture is right now and how promising the future looks, we must remember: There is an enemy out there who wants to destroy God's Church!

What should you do if demonic devourers attack your field? *Start a fire and release some Holy Ghost smoke!*

There is no other counterattack to deal with a demonic infestation. Satan knows how to start so many crises, he can keep you running from one problem to another, another, and another. The problem is, all the wise counsel in the world, your best intentions, and your earnest desire and hard work *aren't* going to repel a satanic attack.

You might say, "I know! I'll call the prayer warriors together and they will put an end to this problem." Thank God for prayer warriors, but when a major demonic attack occurs, there aren't enough prayer warriors in the land to deal with a large invasion of demonic troops.

Even if you could get enough believers together to do combat (the first miracle would be getting them together!), it would probably be too late.

In our society, it takes time to get people together. It takes time to get people to "agree" about "what" they should "agree for in prayer."

Everyone seems to think he or she should voice an opinion about "the real problem," speak their own insight about how to combat the attack, and teach their particular revelation about how the problem started and who is to blame for letting the devil into our camp! By the time our ranks finally get together and find a point of agreement, the damage is already severe.

Instead, we must learn to turn up the fire of the Holy Spirit! *Demon spirits hate Holy Ghost smoke!*

Rather than worry, fret, or handle these attacks from man's point of view, let us release the smoke of the Holy Ghost! As Zechariah 4:6 says, "Not by might, nor by power, but by my spirit, saith the Lord of hosts."

## Turn the Fire Up

Satanic attacks on your fields, the Church, your ministry, your family, or perhaps your business, must be dealt with by fire and smoke.

This is a time for you to let the fire of the Spirit burn more brilliantly than ever before. And, if the attacks against you are large, this means you must build a bigger fire. The larger the attack, the larger the fire that is required. If the attack is small, then less fire is needed to combat the attack.

With the fire of the Holy Spirit blazing hot within us, we must release the smothering smoke of the Spirit into the spirit realm, to suffocate the demonic presence and drive them out of our camps.

*If they refuse to leave, fine! Let them fall out of the spirit realm, suffocating in God's overwhelming power as they hurl downward to their destruction, right into the Holy Spirit's fire, to be burned until they are totally consumed.*

The choice is before them. The options for them are: flee in terror from the Spirit's smoke, or be totally consumed in God's wrath. Remember, "our God is a consuming fire" (Hebrews 12:29).

Absolutely nothing is more effective in turning away demonic attack than to release a strong, hot blaze of the Spirit's fire and His powerful, suffocating smoke. This Holy Ghost smoke will ensure the safety of your harvest!

## God Says, "This Is a Must!"

In Paul's statement to Timothy, he says, "The husbandman that laboureth *must be* first partaker of the fruits."

Notice the phrase "must be." Why? Because Paul is telling us something that absolutely, positively *MUST BE!* In other words, the point he is about to make is not an option; it is a *necessity.*

"Must be" in Greek is the word *dei* (pronounced like "day"). It is always used to convey the idea of an obligation, a necessity, a requirement, a demand, or a rule to never, never be broken — a rule to which there is absolutely no (not even a tiny) exception.

What is this *demand* God is making? What is the *necessity* spoken of here? What is so important, crucial, and vital that this rule can never bend, be modified, or be altered?

Paul tells us, "The husbandman that laboureth *must be first partaker of the fruits.*"

## God's Promise to You Personally

What you find in Second Timothy 2:6 is a personal promise to you from God!

Because Paul says, "The husbandman that laboureth *must be. . .,*" he is telling us something that absolutely must be! Because the phrase "must be" is the Greek word dei, which speaks of *a necessity,* you could translate it, "The husbandman that laboureth *absolutely must be. . . .*" Or, "The husbandman that laboureth *is totally obligated and under command. . . .*"

What is the obligation referred to in this verse?

Paul says, "The husbandman that laboureth must be *first partaker of the fruits.*" In other words, God wants the committed, determined, hard-working combat zone fighter to eat from the table of victory and to enjoy the fruit of success *before* anyone else does!

This is God's promise to combat zone fighters!

When you look at the entire text of Second Timothy 2:3-6, you understand that God is saying, *"If you fight like a soldier. . . if you prepare and train like an athlete. . . if you give your heart and soul to your field of ministry like a farmer. . . here is what I will do for you. . .*

*"I am fixing it permanently — a rule to never be changed, altered, or modified — and I am making it a top priority and necessity, that when your battle is over, and you've proven yourself a good soldier; when your spiritual competition is defeated and you've exercised hard like an athlete; when your crop begins to grow and mature before your eyes —* YOU WILL EAT BEFORE ANYONE ELSE EATS!"

The thought continues, *"I will make sure you partake of the blessings! In fact, I have decided you will be the first partaker of the fruits. You've done the fighting, training, and work; therefore, it is fitting that you should taste the fruits before anyone else."*

Isn't that good news?

God wants you to eat the fruit of your labors and enjoy it. It would be ridiculous for a local pastor to pour all his life into his church and then never taste any victory. It would be ridiculous for an apostle, prophet, evangelist, or teacher to travel and give his or her life to the Body of Christ and then never see any wonderful fruit produced as a result of it.

Just like a Roman soldier was rewarded for a good combat fight, you *will be* rewarded for your fight in the combat zone!

In the same way a Greek athlete was rewarded for his training and facing his competition victoriously, you *will be* crowned with tremendous blessings for facing demonic competition and adversity.

Like a hard-working farmer who gives his life to see fruit grow in his field, when you work your land and labor strenuously to make God's Word grow in hearts, in the midst of the combat zone, *God promises you will eat the fruit!*

## When Do You Get Rewarded?

Are the blessings of God reserved only for heaven? No, of course not. While eternal rewards do await faithful Christian soldiers, many blessings are ready to be delivered to the saints *now!*

Roman soldiers didn't risk their lives so they could be killed and later compensated. They did it so they could be rewarded during their lifetime!

Likewise, the Greek athletes of Timothy's day didn't do all that training, work, and preparation in order to die without reward. They were after the reward, and desired immediate gratification for their skill and work.

Farmers didn't do their farming so the crop would fail! They planned on reaping a harvest as soon as possible. They made this their goal every year. They were after the fruit of the field!

*Is it wrong or carnal to desire reward?*

*Is it wrong or carnal to want recognition for your fight?*

*It is wrong or carnal to reach for blessings in this life?*

*Is it wrong or carnal to expect remuneration for your labors?*

No! That is exactly what Paul is trying to tell us. If you have done your job well, you should expect to be rewarded, recognized, blessed, and remunerated for your efforts! Anyone who lives, fights, and conquers in the combat zone should be rewarded!

It's just like Jesus said:

> **Verily I say unto you, There is no man that hath left house, or brethren, or sisters, or father, or mother, or wife, or children, or lands, for my sake, and the gospel's.**
>
> **But he shall receive an hundredfold now in this time, houses, and brethren, and sisters, and mothers, and children, and lands, with persecutions; and in the world to come eternal life.**
>
> **Mark 10:29,30**

Religious spirits try to tell us to expect nothing back in this life for our service. This thinking says all rewards are spiritual only, and are bestowed only in heaven. In fact, these same religious spirits tell us our motives are wrong and we are in sin, if we expect to be rewarded now with temporal blessings for our efforts.

This thinking says we should never give tithes and offerings with a thought of receiving back, and we should never serve in any capacity with a hidden thought of being rewarded.

This is wrong!

Paul said:

> **Who goeth a warfare any time at his own charges? who planteth a vineyard, and eateth not of the fruit thereof? or who feedeth a flock, and eateth not of the milk of the flock?**
>
> **Say I these things as a man? or saith not the law the same also?**
>
> **For it is written in the law of Moses, Thou shalt not muzzle the mouth of the ox that treadeth out the corn. Doth God take care for oxen?**
>
> **Or saith he it altogether for our sakes? For our sakes, no doubt, this is written: that he that ploweth should plow in hope; and that he that thresheth in hope should be partaker of his hope.**
>
> **If we have sown unto you spiritual things, is it a great thing if we shall reap your carnal things?**
>
> **1 Corinthians 9:7-11**

Warriors *deserve* blessings! Good athletes *deserve* recognition. Farmers *deserve* to eat their crops. And if *you* are living and fighting your fight of faith in the combat zone, *you deserve a big victory!* And not only a spiritual reward in heaven, but a tangible, measurable piece of success right now — just like any warrior, athlete, or farmer should expect!

This is why God has fixed it for you to be rewarded for your fight! Once again, in Second Timothy 2:6, Paul says, "The husbandman that laboureth *must be first partaker of the fruits.*" Any other prospect would be unfair and wrong to the worker.

## Did Paul Really Say That?

In First Corinthians 9:24, Paul says, "Know ye not that they which run in a race run all, but one receiveth the prize? So run, that ye may obtain."

Notice especially where Paul says, ". . . run, that ye may obtain." The word "obtain" is the Greek word *katalambano* (ka-ta-lam-ba-no). It refers to "a conquering attitude." It means "to grab hold of something, pull it down, subdue it, and make it your very own!" It is the idea of *dominion.*

Paul's attitude was a conquering attitude. He was running, fighting, serving, and working in order to *obtain.* He wanted to conquer, subdue, and obtain in every area of life! His desire was *dominion* in every area of life. What specific example did he use in this verse? A runner, or *an athlete!*

If an athlete should expect to obtain, then we should expect to obtain, too. Paul continued in this athletic mode by saying, "And every man that striveth for the mastery is temperate in all things. Now they do it to obtain a corruptible crown, but we an incorruptible" (v. 25).

Paul says the athletes were temperate in order *"to obtain."* Were those athletes carnal and wrong to expect a reward? No, it is simply logical that an athlete should be rewarded! No one would question this. Well, we should expect to receive, too! And not only an incorruptible crown in heaven, but a tangible, physical reward as well *right now in this life.*

We should expect to receive immediate results for our labor. We combat zone fighters are destined to have the best of both worlds.

What was Paul's personal motto for life? "Run that ye may obtain!"

## Prescription for Supernatural Revelation

Has the Holy Spirit ever said anything to you that was a little difficult to understand? Did your mind have trouble comprehending what God was trying to say to you?

That is why Paul says, "Consider what I say; and the Lord give thee understanding in all things" (2 Timothy 2:7).

Timothy was having trouble putting all of Paul's message together. First, Paul says to act like a soldier. Then, it seems Paul switches and tells Timothy to view himself as an athlete. Then, just as quick, he seems to waver in his example again. Now he tells Timothy to be a farmer!

What if you received a letter from me in which I told you to be a soldier, an athlete, and a farmer; I didn't stop to fully explain each point; and I made these vastly different statements in the space of three sentences. You might be a little stunned, too!

Knowing he has given Timothy a lot to think about, Paul says, "*Consider* what I say. . . ."

The word "consider" is the Greek word *noieo* (noi-eo), which comes from the root word *nous* (pronounced "noous"), which is the word "mind." The word "consider," which is from this same root, means "think about this," or "use your mind."

Perhaps it would be better understood as, "You need to think and ponder about these things." Really, the tense indicates a habitual action: "Think, think, think, think, think, think, and think about these things."

Why? Because it was going to take some real sorting out for Timothy to comprehend everything Paul has said. Each statement he made was packed full of deep meaning, was dramatically different from the previous one, and was vital for Timothy to understand.

If he read this letter from Paul too quickly, he would miss the deeper message. Therefore, Paul says, "Think about these things. It's time to use your mind. You must ponder everything I've said to you. In fact, you need to think, think, think, and think about them."

It is not wrong to use your brain. God gave you a marvelous mind, and He wants you to *use* it. Many Spirit-filled people think it is carnal or unspiritual to be a "thinker." This is contrary to scripture.

A Spirit-filled person should "think" better than anyone else does! The Holy Spirit never brings stupidity or silliness. Rather, the Holy Spirit always brings "enlightenment." He brings "revelation," "insight," and "illumination." Don't view your mind as carnality, or try to symbolically take your mind out and set it on some back shelf. God gave you your brain, and He wants you to use it.

People are always asking me, "Rick, how did you get so much revelation about God's Word? How does God show you truths in the scriptures?" It is really quite simple: I use my brain!

You may say, "What? Come on — tell us more!" In addition to prayer in the Spirit and exercising my faith, I use my mind. I open my Bible, pull out my study books, history books, and Greek New Testament, and I start *thinking*. I think, think, think, and think. In fact, sometimes I think so hard, my head begins to hurt! Then a miracle occurs!

Paul says, "Consider what I say; *and the Lord give thee understanding in all things*." What is the miracle? God-imparted, supernatural understanding.

Here is how the miracle works. And here is my part and your part to receive supernatural understanding. Here it is: think, think, think, think, think, think about the Word, and then start thinking, thinking, thinking, thinking, and thinking, and then you must consider, ponder, and roll it over, over, and over again in your mind.

This is *our part* — to bend our mind and submit it to discipline. And as we use our minds, the miracle takes place: "The Lord will give thee *understanding* in all things."

Look at the beauty of this! You are using your normal, God-given brain, and you are thinking and thinking and thinking. For me personally, I am pulling Greek words apart. I am studying the language. I am studying writers. I am studying this book and that book, and I am thinking and thinking.

Then, all of a sudden, a thought will come into my mind. It's *not* a thought of my own; it comes from the Holy Spirit. Suddenly, in the midst of doing my part — praying, thinking, and studying — God gives me *understanding.*

The Greek word for "understanding" is the word *sunesis* (su-ne-sis). It describes "a coming together of all the parts." This means if we will use our minds and get into a position to hear from God, He will speak to our minds, and will bring all the difficult-to-understand pieces of information together like the pieces of a jigsaw puzzle. He will bring it all together, and when He does, you'll be able to see clearly what He has to say to you. This is *understanding.*

Have you ever needed vital information from God? Perhaps you had a piece of direction, and maybe even another little piece. However, you couldn't seem to "piece them together." Your own human perception of God's plan was fragmented, and you couldn't make sense of it. When this happens, it's time to use your mind and think!

Bend your mind to the Word. Make your mind work hard, and consider what the scripture has to say to you. If you do your part, a supernatural understanding will begin to emerge. God will drive a thought into your mind that will "put it all together for you." It is *understanding.*

## For Fighters Only

What does this have to do with you? How does this relate to the combat zone you're living in right now?

You, like Timothy, must spend time meditating and thinking about the examples Paul has given us. You won't fully comprehend it all at once. Therefore, you must be constantly thinking, thinking, thinking, and thinking about these things. You can't ponder on this enough.

If we bend our minds and think hard — if we submit our thinking to God's plan, and start viewing ourselves as militant, warring soldiers, as serious athletes in training, and immerse ourselves fully into the work of the field like farmers — we will come through our current combat zone as champions!

Take Paul's advice and "Think about it." If you do, the Lord will show you revelation beyond your wildest expectation. He'll give you "understanding in all of these things."

## Chapter 9
# The Choice Is Ours To Make

The choice to win or lose a fight in the combat zone is ours to make! God will not make us fight. If we wish, He will permit us to *lose!*

Losing is obviously *not* God's will for our lives. However, because God allows freedom of choice, He will allow us to make decisions for ourselves. Our choices are: Get in the fight and slug it out, or shut our eyes and pretend the enemy isn't there!

If we win the fight, it is because we *decided* to fight. If we lose the fight, we must face this fact: We didn't fight like we should have; therefore, we lost. All of us eat the fruit of our own decision and choice.

How unfortunate it will be for us, especially in the present hour, if we say to ourselves, "Well, this militant mentality was fine for the first century believers. They had to think this way just in order to survive. While I can understand why they had to think that way, I'm not that committed yet.

"You see, I'm not up against the wall the way they were. We're not being persecuted for our faith. We live in a nation where it is easy to serve the Lord. I don't like to think about all that warfare business! That sounds hard! Besides, to really live and think like this would cramp my lifestyle! I'd have to do a lot of changing. And I'm not willing to do that right now. Maybe later."

## Doomed by a Wrong Decision

If this is our way of thinking, we are *doomed* — and not by the devil or demonic attack, but by our own *lack of commitment!*

It is true that Satan is against the Church. Yes, it's true that he wants to discredit it, scandalize television ministries, damage fivefold ministry gifts, throw church leaders into rebellion, immoral situations, or hurtful circumstances, wreck the kingdom's finances, scatter the flock, and hurl us into spiritual bankruptcy. He wants to steal our end-time opportunity to reach a lost world for Jesus Christ!

Furthermore, he wants to keep brothers and sisters divided, angry, and at odds with each other, and keep leaders in disagreement with each other over petty, insignificant issues. He knows what the Church can do if She ever unites together in the Spirit!

The devil, perhaps more than even we ourselves, knows that the Church has the power and might of Almighty God! Therefore, Satan is constantly working to throw this beloved army of the Lord into confusion and disarray. He tries to keep us marching in a disorderly fashion.

Clearly, Satan's plan to attack and victimize the Church has worked, to some extend. Yet he can do absolutely none of this *unless* we permit him to.

How do we *permit* the devil to do this? By remaining quiet, stationary, on the back row, uncommitted, spiritually lazy, unexercised, unprepared, and untrained to fight.

*By taking a neutral stand and sitting on the fence, we are making our decision to lose!* By doing nothing — no warring, fighting, or mental training — we are choosing to let the devil win the war in the combat zone.

## What If the Fight Gets Hard

If your combat zone gets intense and hard, then you must be *harder!* That is why Paul previously said, "Endure hardness as a good soldier of Jesus Christ" (2 Timothy 2:3).

Someone nearly always says, "Yes, I know it says to be a good soldier like Jesus Christ. But be honest. Come on! Can anyone *really* be the kind of soldier that Jesus Christ was? I mean, He was God! How could anyone fight as bravely as Jesus did? If I was God, like He was, it would be easier to fight!"

If this is the way you're thinking, you're *wrong!* However, this may be the very way that Timothy was thinking after reading Paul's letter. Timothy may have thought like we do: "This sounds hard! Can any man or woman be all of these things? Is there anyone in the world besides Jesus Himself that can be so committed?"

That is why Paul continues in Second Timothy 2:8, "Remember that Jesus Christ of the seed of David was raised from the dead according to my gospel."

## Does Anyone Understand Your Problem?

Notice the above verse covers four specific areas related to the person of Jesus Christ. These four areas are: (1) *Remember,* (2) *His humanity,* (3) *His resurrection,* and (4) *the Gospel message.*

Why does Paul now start telling us to remember Jesus Christ, then His humanity, His resurrection, and the Gospel? Because these four subjects will encourage Timothy's heart!

In the first place, the Word says, "*Remember* Jesus Christ. . . ." The word "remember" is the Greek word *mnemoneuo* (mne-mo-neuo), which is the root for "a grave, tomb, sepulchre, statue, memorial, or monument." It is the same word which Paul used in chapter one, verse three, when he said, "I have remembrance of thee in my prayers night and day." (We covered this in Chapter 1 of this book.)

By selecting this word, it tells us Timothy has *lost sight* of something very important. What did he lose sight of? Jesus Christ!

Timothy's ministry in Ephesus had been such a challenge that he had lost touch with some important things. He was so consumed by his own pastoral and personal troubles, he *forgot* about the trial that Jesus Himself had gone through. He *forgot* about Jesus' victory over the grave! All he could see or think about was negative — defeat, failure, sorrow, and rejection. You might say Timothy was *swamped!*

Now, after giving Timothy these strong admonitions about life in the combat zone, he suddenly tells Timothy to "remember Jesus Christ. . . ." Why? Because Timothy is operating under a spirit of fear. He is giving way to wild emotions and is so depressed, he can hardly lift his head.

He wanted to hear Paul *pamper* him! He wanted Paul to *feel sorry* for him! He wanted someone to *coddle* him and tell him it would somehow all work out. What does Paul do instead? Paul tells him to get up, make a decision to forgive, fight, be empowered, and then get back on the front lines of battle!

What was Timothy's reaction to Paul's letter? A typical flesh response! "Oh, yeah? You obviously don't understand me or my problems, Paul. If you knew what I was going through, you'd talk nicer to me! Instead, you tell me to stay in there and keep on fighting as though nothing has happened.

"*You've* clearly never been through *this* kind of trouble, or you would understand and be more compassionate! My situation is *different*. It's *special*. No one, absolutely no one, has ever been through this kind of situation before!"

## Have You Lost Sight of Jesus Christ?

That is why Paul says, "*Remember* Jesus Christ. . . ." No one, including Paul, Timothy, or any other person, has ever gone through the ordeal the Lord Jesus Christ endured! Yet He survived it and won the ultimate war for all of us!

Thus, Paul says, "Remember. . . ." Because the word "remember" can be translated "grave, tomb, or sepulchre, it means Timothy's accurate vision of Jesus had become blurred — or perhaps even almost forgotten. Therefore, Paul commands him to "remember," or "Dig through your swamped mind like a grave covered with dirt, and pull out a clear vision of Jesus Christ!"

In fact, this word "remember" is the present active imperative, which means it could be translated, "I'm not *suggesting* you remember this. I'm *commanding* you to remember it. In fact, I want you to remember, remember, remember, remember, and remember it. You keep calling this to memory, and don't you ever forget it again!"

Paul tells him to resurrect an accurate picture of Jesus Christ, and then to erect it like a statue, monument, or memorial. Where was he to erect this monument? *In his mind.* He was to build a lasting, permanent vision of all Jesus Christ endured, and he was to build a fixed image in his mind of a Lord who conquered every foe. Why? For the sake of encouragement!

No one has been through the trial Jesus went through. Our problems look weak when you consider the cruel trial, scourgings, mocking, and horrible death that Jesus endured. Then, to add more to His hideous death, He spent three days in hell itself!

## Have You Ever Spent Three Days in Hell?

The cross was no joy ride! Hebrews 12:2 says, "Looking unto Jesus, the author and finisher of our faith; who for the joy that was set before him endured the cross, despising the shame, and is set down at the right hand of the throne of God."

Notice it didn't say, "who loved hanging on the cross, and enjoyed the shame. . . ."

Instead, the Word says, "He endured the cross." The word "endure" is the Greek word *hupomeno* (hu-po-meno), and indicates "a commitment to stay in one spot, regardless of how hard or difficult it gets." In other words, the word "endure" tells us the cross was no joy ride!

But Jesus was committed to stay right there, hanging on that horrible cross, regardless of the personal torment it brought Him, or the price He had to pray.

To tell us what Jesus thought of this cross, the verse continues, "*despising* the shame. . . ." The word "despising" is the Greek word *kataphroneo* (ka-ta-phro-neo), which means "to look down on something, to disdain an object, to feel humiliated about something, to scorn, or to have contempt for something."

This clearly tells us Jesus did not "enjoy the shame." He *despised* His work on the cross — *disdained* it as an object of scorn; had *contempt* for this ugly assignment; and was *humiliated* by its condemnation of Him.

His distaste for the work of His cross was so strong that the Word says, "despising the *shame*. . . . " The word "shame" in Greek is the word *aischunos* (ai-schu-nos), which is the word for "a disgraceful predicament."

Jesus saw His public nakedness, public ridicule, slanderous trial, and absorption of man's sin as a disgrace to Himself. The idea of three days in hell was a horrendous thought, even to Jesus.

Then why did Jesus do it? Hebrews 12:2 says He did it because of "the joy that was set before him. . .and is [now] set down at the right hand of the throne of God."

Once again, why did Jesus go through all this? He did all of this *for us* and *for Himself!* He did it for "the joy that was set before him." He had His eyes set (permanently *fixed)* on His reward!

Therefore, He was committed to go through this whole gamut of devilish ordeals to obtain His rightful place at the Father's right hand. Imagine the *joy* Jesus experienced when He passed out of hell's embrace and received His place of authority!

What is "the joy set before *you*" today? A successful church? A music ministry? A prophetic, teaching, or traveling ministry? A growing business? Or perhaps a saved family or family member?

Just like Jesus, you must keep your eye permanently fixed on your desire! If your vision wavers, you will begin to let loose of your commitment. That is the time to hold tight! You must sternly look forward, staring at your goal. Jesus fixed His sight on the glory, and the hope before Him *enabled* Him to endure the cross and its shame. Therefore, be like Jesus and keep your eyes fixed on "the joy set before you"!

## Jesus Sang a Solo!

In order to grasp the sensation of victory Jesus Himself felt when He conquered all His enemies, look at Colossians 2:15. The Word says, "And having spoiled principalities and powers, he made a shew of them openly, triumphing over them in it."

This is what I call a *graphic* verse. It is *a picture* painted for us by the Holy Spirit — a gorgeous, vivid *illustration* of something very important: the day Jesus defeated death, hell, and the grave!

The phrase "triumphing over them in it" is the key to this verse. This phrase is from the Greek word *triambeuo* (tri-am-beuo), which is a technical word used to describe a general or an emperor who was returning home from a grand victory in the enemy's territory. The word "triumph" *(triambeuo)* was a specific word used to describe this emperor's *triumphal parade!*

When news reached the city that the enemy had been defeated, plans for a triumphal parade immediately went into action. By the time the gates of the city were opened wide to receive this emperor who was now returning home in triumph, his people were ready to celebrate his victory!

As the gates swung open and this mighty warrior rode through, *the celebration began!*

Sitting astride a large, beautiful, white stallion, draped in his kingly, regal garments, and wearing his bright and shining royal crown upon his head, the returning emperor led the entire city in a procession of celebration and victory. It was called his "triumphal parade."

As he rode down the main avenue of the city with his head held high, his shoulders thrown back, and a look of victory on his face, the city began rejoicing. *"He's back! He's back! Our king has won a massive victory!"* People would break into dancing, singing, and jubilantly hurling themselves in circles. This was a time to rejoice!

In order to flaunt his great victory, the returning victor would parade behind him the foreign king, taken in captivity. There, behind the victor, walked the defeated foe bound in heavy chains of bondage. Behind this defunct foe walked the defeated king's ruling men and leaders, now bound and chained along with their ruined king.

Further back behind them were oxcarts loaded to overflowing with booty taken *by force* from the enemy's homeland. Once these goods had belonged to the enemy, but now they belonged to the conquering king!

As the returning, victorious emperor rode down the avenue, he strutted with pride, flaunting his defeated foes, and "made a show of them openly." He wanted everyone to see the fabulous goods he had stolen from his enemy's hand! The enemy had been completely "spoiled."

But it doesn't stop here!

*The entire celebration began when the emperor sang a song of victory! As he rode that horse through the gate, leading his triumphal parade, he would open his mouth and sing as loud as he could sing! With all of his might, he would sing, "The enemy is defeated. . . the foe is conquered. . . let it be known that I am still king!"*

This song would throw the crowd into a frenzy. This was the voice and this was the song they were waiting for! The king had returned, and he was *still king!*

Then, after riding down the main avenue, revealing his booty, and singing his song of victory, the victor stopped in front of a large set of stairs which led upward to a huge, ornate throne. His military conquest proved that he was still the holder of authority. Therefore, he proudly walked up those steps, turned toward the crowd, and lowered himself down into the seat, sitting in his rightful place, *the throne.*

All of this is *the background* to Colossians 2:15, which says, "And having spoiled principalities and powers, he made a shew of them openly, triumphing over them in it."

This was "the joy that was set before him"! Once death, hell, and the grave were conquered, Jesus returned home to heaven where a celebrative, triumphal parade took place! Who led the parade? The Victor, Jesus Christ!

What song did He sing? Perhaps it went something like this: "I've defeated the enemy. . . Death no longer has a hold on men. . . Satan is completely conquered. . . And let it be known: I AM STILL KING!"

Imagine the worship, praise, and adoration that took place the day that Jesus, our reigning King, returned home to glory to sit down at the Father's right hand!

This celebration, worship, and grand victory were *the reason Jesus could "endure the cross."* He didn't "enjoy the shame"; He "despised the shame." However, the eternal rewards far outweighed the temporal, momentary suffering of the cross.

## Remember, Remember, Remember. . .

Paul's command to Timothy is to "Remember Jesus Christ. . . ." Because it is the present active imperative, it really is a command: *"I command you to remember, and to be constantly remembering. . ."*

Why? Because Timothy feels like he is never going to get out of his war zone! It looks like everything is falling apart, and there is no hope of restoration. Thus, Paul tells Timothy to reflect on the *hell* Jesus endured, and to remember that although the cross was hard, the cross was not the end for Jesus!

Likewise, some of you may currently be carrying a cross or a situation that you despise. Yet, you know you are called to your place of ministry. You know you're in the right place, and you know you're *exactly* where God wants you. But all *hell* seems to be breaking out around you, and you have every rational reason to back out and retreat.

Rather than stopping now, try *"remembering Jesus Christ."* You must reflect on Him: the trial that He endured; the cross that He despised; the disgrace that He felt; and the phenomenal victory that He won!

As Hebrews 12:3 says, "For consider him that endured such contradiction of sinners against himself, lest ye be wearied and faint in your minds."

The word "consider" used here is the Greek word *analogidzomai* (ana-lo-gid-zo-mai), which means "to think again; to reflect on that subject one more time." It conveys the idea of *habitual meditation*. It is again the imperative, which tells us this is not a suggestion, but a *command*.

The idea of the word is "think, think, and think again; reflect on this subject one more additional time; don't stop; instead, go ahead and do it habitually. As a matter of fact, I command you to do this."

*By meditating on Jesus Christ and all that He "endured," we become strong to face our own fight of faith*. The word "endure" is the same Greek word used in Hebrews 12:2, and again indicates a commitment to stay in one spot, regardless of how hard or difficult it gets.

By using this word a *second* time, the Holy Spirit is laying emphasis on this point. He wants us to know the cross was not enjoyable, but something to be "endured." But because it was part of Jesus' necessary journey to win the war for our lives, He endured it. It was hard, but He was "committed to stay in that place, regardless of how hard or difficult it became." Thank God for Jesus' relentless commitment!

But there is something else extremely important here in Hebrews 12:3. It says, "For consider him that endured such *contradiction* of sinners against himself. . . ."

Notice the word "contradiction." In Greek, it is the word *antilogia* (anti-lo-gia), a compound of the two words *anti* and *logia*.

The word *anti* means "against," and conveys the idea of hostility, and the word *logia* simply means "words." When compounded, it means, "angry, hostile, cruel words."

It is amazing that when Jesus took His greatest step of faith and literally laid His life on the altar of sacrifice, *that* is when His most slanderous persecution arose! There, hanging on that cross, Luke 23:35 records, "And the people stood beholding. And the rulers also with them derided him, saying, He saved others; let him save himself, if he be the Christ, the chosen of God."

Verses 36 and 37 continue, "And the soldiers also mocked him. . . saying, If thou be the king of the Jews, save thyself." Verse 39 adds another insult: "And one of the malefactors which were hanged railed on him, saying, If thou be Christ, save thyself and us."

In Jesus' greatest hour of pain, what did He receive? Insults and abusive comments!

## Has This Been Your Experience?

Have you ever felt like you were being "talked about," or "laughed at," or "railed," because of your fight of faith? Has this been your experience, too?

If so, you're doing something right! Hebrews 10:32 says all faithful fighters experience this kind of ridicule. The Word says, "But call to remembrance the former days, in which, after ye were illuminated, ye endured a great fight of afflictions."

Notice the word "illuminated." It is the Greek word *photidzo* (pho-tid-zo), which refers to "light, enlightenment, or fresh revelation." It is where we get the first part of the word "*photo*graph." The idea is that this new illumination, or light, is so powerful, it has left a *permanent, lasting impression on your life.*

Can you remember when you were "illuminated" concerning the infilling of the Holy Spirit? Didn't it feel like someone suddenly "turned the light on" for you? Did it leave a lasting mark on your life?

Do you remember when you heard for the first time that Jesus Christ "took your infirmities and carried your diseases"? Do you recall how your spirit seemed to burst forth with joy? Why did you feel this way? Because you had become "illuminated." Did it leave a permanent impression on your life?

Can you recall the day when you were first called into the ministry? The Holy Spirit "illuminated" you about the call of God. What happened to you? Were you overwhelmed, filled with joy, and forever changed?

Real "illumination" from the Holy Spirit makes a strong mark on our lives. It forever changes us. And it's a good thing, because look what follows "illumination." The Word says, "in which, after ye were illuminated, *ye endured a great fight of afflictions.*"

## Look What Follows Illumination!

What follows "illumination"? Look at the verse again: "...after ye were illuminated, *ye endured a great fight of afflictions.*" A fight always follows illumination!

The word "endured" is once again the word *hupomeno* (hu-po-meno). This tells us, regardless of how hard the fight becomes, we must make the decision to stand in faith and be immovable in our commitment.

But look at what it says we must endure: "a great fight of afflictions." Notice there are three important words used here: "great," "fight," and "afflictions."

The word "great" is the Greek word *mega* (me-ga), which describes something very, very large. It is where we get the word "*mega*phone," which describes an instrument for making a very, very loud noise.

This word *mega* is why people speak of "*mega*-bills," *mega*-problems, *mega*-work," and so forth. The word *mega* speaks of "enlargement." By using this word, this verse tells us the fight that follows illumination is not normally small; rather, it is normally *mega*.

The next important word in the verse is the word "fight." This word is the Greek word *athlesis* (ath-le-sis), which refers to "a committed athlete," like the Greek athletes we saw in Chapter 8. Because this word is used in this context, it conveys the message that real, powerful illumination may throw you into the greatest challenge of your entire life!

Finally we come to the word "afflictions," which is the Greek word *pathema* (pa-the-ma). This word *pathema* primarily refers to "mental pressure," or suffering that affects *the mind*. This is *not* a reference to mental sickness, however. Instead, it refers to a fight of faith; a war in your soul; an attack on your mind.

You can be sure of it: If you take a stand in faith, every possible thought will come against your mind! This is what happened to Jesus on the cross. After yielding to the work of the cross and giving His own life selflessly, the soldiers and other criminals began to throw "contradictions" at Him.

Because the Lord Jesus was also humanity, you can be sure He was tempted to listen to their accusations. However, He shoved aside the demonic attack in His soul and endured — "stayed in His place regardless of how hard or difficult it became."

Have you ever been through a *mega-ordeal?*

Have you ever been thrown into *the greatest fight of your life?*

Do you know what it is like to withstand a *mental attack?*

Great! That means you have been *illuminated!* If there was no illumination, there would be no challenge. That fight is *evidence* you're on the right track.

## You're on Center Stage

Hebrews 10:33 continues, "Partly, whilst ye were made a gazingstock both by reproaches and afflictions. . . ."

Notice the word "gazingstock." It is the Greek word *theatron* (thea-tron), from which we get the word "theater." A better translation would be, "You were made a theatre. . ." Or, "You became a spectacle of entertainment. . ." Or, "On account of your stand of faith, you became the best show in town. . ."

It is a picture of spectators taking a seat at the theater to watch how the play goes. They watch Act I, Act II, Act III, and Act IV. However, this audience isn't watching to see how *good* the show is; they are watching in order to catch the players *make a mistake.*

This crowd is on the edge of their seat, anticipating the first mistake, forgotten line, or error on the part of the actors. And when they hear a mistake, they intend to laugh at the player, scorn him, ridicule him, and make fun of him.

This kind of scorn *always* accompanies a stand in faith. There are always spectators who stand by, ready to laugh at you, or to say, "We told you so!" when you make your first mistake in your walk of faith. Unfortunately, many times these spectators are not unbelievers, but *believers!*

The point is, when you take a step of faith or take a new stand on the Word — when you are first illuminated — it will throw you into *public life,* like it or not. You may not be known by thousands, but your life will become dinner conversation among friends, family, associates, and foes.

Everyone will seem to develop an opinion as to whether or not you'll be able to fulfill your dream.

Verse 33 used two other very important words: "reproaches" and "afflictions" (a different word for "afflictions" from the one previously used).

The word "reproach" is the Greek word *oneidismos* (o-nei-dis-mos), and refers to "insults hurled at you from other people." This is precisely what they did to Jesus when He was on the cross. That cross literally put Jesus on the center stage of the Universe. Rather than applauding Him, they "reproached" Him, and threw insults and slanderous statements at Him.

Satan hates a strong stand on God's Word, and he will do everything within his ability to *coax* you off that stand of faith. He'll use family members, friends, associates, and even circumstances to thwart the plan of God for your life.

If you are "illuminated" that you're doing God's perfect will, however, don't budge an *inch* on account of any opposition!

Then the Bible used the word "afflictions." This word is different from the one used in verse 32. This is the Greek word *thlipsis* (thlip-sis), which refers to a tight squeeze, or *incredible pressure.* This is what life does to you!

It is bad enough to have revilers against you, but the Word says life itself will try to come against you when you take a stand in faith. The word *thlipsis* indicates everything around you will try to shut down on you when you are illuminated.

You see, the devil hates the illumination in your heart. All of these problems are not indicators that you're doing something wrong; they indicate instead that you're doing something *right!* He hates you *because* you are illuminated.

Why is "illumination" so terrifying to Satan? Because an "illuminated" person is a dangerous person! *Such a person knows that he knows that he knows that he knows that he knows — and he doesn't care if anyone else in the world agrees with him or not!* This is a person who religious politics cannot buy and Satan cannot stop.

Spiritual illumination is a powerful force. The person who has been illuminated will stand in faith against all the odds, and he will *beat them!* This individual will oppose the opinion of the entire world if he must, because *he knows* he's right!

However, you must know in advance, a fight will always follow illumination.

## "Lest Ye Be Wearied..."

It is important for us to know all of this "lest ye be wearied and faint in your minds" (Hebrews 12:3).

The word "weary" is the word *kamete* (ka-me-te), which describes "someone who is slowly being worn out." He has tried and tried to remain true, but he is slowly feeling *spiritually depleted.*

Notice the next word, "faint." This tells us what will happen to us *if* we give in to weariness. The word "faint" is the word *ekluomai* (ek-luo-mai), a compound of the two words *ek* and *luo. Ek* means "out," and *luo* means "to loosen or lose."

The word *luo* is used in Luke 3:16, where John the Baptist said of Jesus, "...the latchet of whose shoes I am not worthy *to unloose.*" The word "unloose" is this same word *luo,* and means in this sense "to loosen so loosely that the shoes would slip right off."

Compounded together, the word *ek* ("out") and the word *luo* ("loose") describe an individual so weary, tired, and exhausted that he literally "goes limp." You might say he is "out of it." This is a picture of total defeat. One expositor says a modern translation could be to "lose out."

Certainly it is possible to become so spiritually depleted that you no longer care if you win or lose. Spiritual burnout is a possibility. But you need *not* accept either of these options. God has a better way. The Word says "consider him. . . ."

When you become exhausted and tired of living in the combat zone, that is the time to stop and think again about Jesus Himself! When you consider Him — His trials, His death, His days in hell, and the fact that He came out the Winner — your heart will grow strong again, and you will be ready to keep fighting your fight of faith.

## Jesus Christ — Of the Seed of David

Next in Paul's letter to Timothy, he says, "Remember that Jesus Christ *of the seed of David. . . .*" (2 Timothy 2:8). Why does he make the statement "of the seed of David"? Because he wants to place emphasis on *the humanity* of Jesus Christ.

It is almost as though Paul says, "Jesus defeated death, hell, and the grave while He was still the seed of David." Or Paul implies, "Jesus Christ did this not in the power of His Divinity, but *as a man* — just like we are — as "the seed of David."

Why is this important? Because it removes all arguments which say, "Well, He could do it because He was God." Paul attacks that kind of thinking before it has a chance to sprout. Paul makes his message clear: While Jesus Christ *was* God, His marvelous victory over Satan was won while He was still *"of the seed of David."*

This is significant, because it means if Jesus Christ could face His trials, scourgings, mockery, cross, humiliation, and death in the weak power of the flesh — as *a man* — and still come out the victor, then we can face our combat zone and come out the victor, too!

Therefore, we have *no* excuses! We can't blame our defeat on anyone else or say it was impossible for us to win. Jesus was up against the odds to a degree that our minds cannot comprehend. Still, He remained faithful to the call and accomplished His task!

*Jesus defeated Satan as a man, and so can you!*

## Remember the Resurrection

Paul immediately says, "Remember that Jesus Christ of the seed of David, *was raised from the dead*. . . ." Jesus didn't stay dead; He arose!

Imagine how horrible it would have been if Jesus was assigned to hell forever to maintain our salvation! Thank God, hell and torture was not His final destiny. Neither is the combat zone your home forever!

God's intention for you is resurrection and victory. Like Jesus was raised out from the dead as a living Lord over a defeated foe, God's intention is for you to one day pass out of the combat zone into your victory, never again to be disturbed by your foul foe!

Don't allow the enemy to lie to you and tell you that you are assigned to a life of fighting forever! Such thinking will discourage your heart! *We're fighting not for the sake of fighting, but for the purpose of winning!*

Timothy was swamped in his troubles, and that's all he could see. That is why he was so discouraged. Remember, Jesus Christ was raised from the dead. Just like Jesus, you have a wonderful future in front of you.

Don't give up now; *there is life beyond the combat zone!*

## Do It for the Sake of the Gospel

Then in the last portion of verse 8, Paul says, "Remember that Jesus Christ of the seed of David was raised from the dead *according to my gospel.*" Here, Paul concludes the verse by talking about the Gospel message. Why?

If Timothy can't remain true for any other reason, he must remain true *for the Gospel's sake.* This must be "the bottom line" for all of us.

There were people in Timothy's church who were looking to him as their example. They were watching to see how their fearless leader would respond to the problems around him. He was their example to follow and imitate.

If Timothy forsook the Lord, like others had done, it would have discredited the Gospel message in his church and in the city of Ephesus. Therefore, Paul seems to say, "Timothy, if you can't remain faithful for any other reason, do it for those who are watching. Do it for the sake of the Gospel!

Likewise, you need to be aware that people are watching you. Those same people (spectators) who heard you make your confession of faith are watching you to see if you are *serious.* They are waiting to see if this "faith walk" is *real,* or is just another *passing fancy.* Your example will either *prove* the Gospel to them, or *discredit* it completely. What are you going to do?

Many preachers have prophesied what God was going to do through their church. Then, because of adversity or lack of finances, they backed off and ceased to pursue the vision God gave them.

What a disgrace this is to the Gospel! It brings ridicule and shame upon the preaching of the Word. *If you can't remain true for any other reason, do it for the sake of the Gospel.*

If may be difficult to live a pure life for the Lord after having served the devil for many years. Perhaps you were a drug addict, or were morally loose before your conversion.

After your conversion experience, you shared Jesus Christ with all your old, lost friends. You told them, "Jesus Christ can change your life!"

When you are tempted again by that old sin, and you think about going back into the world, you need to understand your actions may discredit the Gospel and ruin someone else's chance to receive Jesus Christ.

If you go back, your friends are going to say, "Hey, I thought you were a new creature. We knew this 'Christian stuff' would wear out."

Are *you* going to do that to the Gospel? If you can't remain true for any temporal reason, then remain true for *eternal reasons.*

You can make the difference between heaven and hell for some people! You can make the difference between divine healing or premature death for others. Never diminish your importance to the Gospel message. People are watching your life. This is too critical a matter to ignore.

We must never, never lose sight of this crucial consideration. If for no other reason, remain faithful for the sake of the Gospel and those who need it!

## Paul Did It for the Gospel's Sake

That is why Paul continues in Second Timothy 2:9, "Wherein I suffer trouble, as an evil doer, even unto bonds; but the word of God is not bound."

This same Gospel is why Paul is currently imprisoned and the reason he will soon be beheaded. He writes, "Wherein I suffer trouble," or "*This* Gospel is why I suffer trouble." Do you sense his victorious attitude as he concludes with the stirring declaration: ". . . but the word of God is not bound"!

Rather than surrender to his vile predicament, Paul *used* it! He couldn't preach to crowds anymore, but he could write letters. God is able to turn anything around!

*Most of Paul's letters were written as a result of a satanic attack to have him imprisoned.* Because he couldn't physically visit the churches, he addressed them by letter!

It is not a time for you to surrender to the adversary's attacks. *The choice is yours to make; therefore, you must be certain to make the right choice.* Decide to conquer! Decide to win! Decide to use that recent satanic attack as a stepping stone to further the Gospel!

This was Paul's attitude. Concerning his frequent imprisonments, he said:

**But I would ye should understand, brethren, that the things which happened unto me have fallen out rather unto the furtherance of the gospel;**

**So that my bonds in Christ are manifest in all the palace, and in all other places.**

**Philippians 1:12,13**

He could have cried "foul play!" He could have sobbed, "This doesn't line up with my theology!" Or, "Why did God permit this to happen to me?"

Instead of getting bogged in this kind of mental muck, Paul chose to live in victory and use these trials as opportunities. He made *a decision* to live in victory!

And if Paul couldn't remain true for himself or for other temporal reasons, he knew he must remain true for *eternal reasons.* Those people were looking to him for leadership! And there were still those who would sometime in the future come to believe. He had to *decide* to walk in victory *for them.*

Thus, in Second Timothy 2:10, he says, "I endure all things for the elect's sakes, that they may also obtain the salvation which is in Christ Jesus with eternal glory."

## A Song for Warriors

Have you ever wondered what kind of worship services the first-century Church had? What they did during their praise and worship? How they took offerings? How they prayed for the sick? How loud they prayed in tongues? Or how they flowed with the anointing and the gifts of the Holy Spirit? Imagine the kind of vitality that must have filled their church services!

As we come to the end of Paul's message on warfare, we get a *glimpse* of those early services. *Paul concludes his message to us with a literal song or hymn that the early believers sang when they met together to worship.* (However, it sounds quite different from the songs that we sing today.)

"Hymnic literature" is what the scholars call Second Timothy 2:11-13. In other words, these verses are an *actual quote* of a real New Testament hymn. This was a song sung by Paul, Timothy, probably the apostle John, and thousands of others, too.

When "hymnic literature" is used in the New Testament, it is always from a "hymn" that was well known throughout the Church. These hymns were intended to be more than music; they were tools of instruction which chronicled the *real thinking* of the Early Church.

Paul has been speaking to Timothy in military terms. By using this hymn, Paul is making a statement: *"Timothy, I know how to get you to understand what I'm saying! Do you remember that powerful song your congregation sings every week in Ephesus? You surely must know the one I'm talking about. You know, the one that goes like this..."*

Then Paul quotes this familiar hymn, which says:

> **It is a faithful saying: For if we be dead with him, we shall also live with him:**
>
> **If we suffer, we shall also reign with him: if we deny him, he also will deny us:**
>
> **If we believe not, yet he abideth faithful: he cannot deny himself.**
>
> **2 Timothy 2:11-13**

## Take a Look at These Lyrics!

Look at the first line of the song, "It is a faithful saying: For if we be dead with him, we shall also live with him."

Can you imagine getting together in church to sing about *martyrdom?* This was not allegorical speech; this was *reality* for them! Persecution and death were so imminent, they actually included them in their worship services!

One historian has said, "Let me write the songs for a nation, and I can determine the history of that nation."

In order to better prepare themselves for satanic attack, and to live bravely for the Lord, these believers used every tool available to instill *bravery* into the ranks. One tool they used was *hymns.*

## "If We Be Dead With Him. . . ."

The first line of the song goes, "If we be dead with him. . . ." The phrase "If we be dead with him" is from the Greek word *sunapothnesko* (sun-a-po-th-nes-ko), which refers to a literal "partnership in death with someone else."

The first line of this hymn could be translated, "If we join him as a full-fledged partner in death. . ."

Imagine trying to put *that* to music! Even more, imagine trying to teach those lines to your congregation! Do you think the pop Christian radio stations would give it much air time?

The song goes on, "we shall also live with him." This phrase is based on the Greek word *sudzao* (sud-zao), which conveys the idea of *partnership* once again. This line of the hymn could be translated, "We will join with Him in the same kind of supernatural life He now lives."

Singing this kind of song over and over again worked bravery and warfare into the fiber of the Church! Today we still need songs that produce brave warriors!

Oh, that the Church today was committed enough to sing this type of song *and mean it!* This would be evidence that the army of the Lord was marching forth!

Instead, most people would be offended by such lyrics, and they would refuse to participate in singing it. Others would claim the lyrics were filled with "doubt and unbelief." No, no, no! These lines do not represent unbelief, but rather *powerful faith!*

The lyrics say, "Come hell or high water, we're in this army to stay! If they kill us, that's okay; we'll join Jesus in His glorious resurrection!"

## "If We Suffer. . . ."

The next line of the song says, "If we suffer, we shall also reign with him." The phrase "if we suffer" in Greek once again unites us to Jesus Christ in *a partnership.* Literally translated, it means, "If we join Him in His suffering and suffer the same way He did. . . ."

Notice there is no note of sorrow or pain about their suffering. Feeling sorry for themselves wouldn't change the situation, so they faced it bravely in the power of the Spirit.

Although they didn't seek to suffer, they were not afraid to suffer *if* it was forced upon them because of their faith. These are the lyrics of a *fearless* people. They were determined to have victory! Therefore, the song continues, "we shall also reign with him."

The phrase "reign with him" is the Greek word *sumbasileuo* (sum-ba-si-leuo), which means "we will reign and rule like a nobility with Him." They had their sights fixed on *ruling with Jesus!* To do this, they would fight any foe.

## "If We Deny Him. . . ."

Now comes the hard part of the song; the part that carries consequences. It says, "If we deny him, he also will deny us."

Can you imagine looking someone straight in the eyes to sing to them, "If you deny the Lord, the Lord will deny you, too"? They definitely had an attitude about Christianity which is missing today!

They saw *no room* for excuses of defectors in the army of the Lord. You were with Him, or you were against Him. Furthermore, they didn't sweep it under the carpet and hide it when a brother defected. Neither did they simply pat him on the back and say, "Well now, come back and visit us sometime."

*They were an ARMY!*

Those who go Absent Without Leave (AWOL) are not worthy of honor or special privileges. Yet, today we comfort defectors and beg and plead with them to come back.

If a brother or a sister has fallen into sin, or is hurt by a relationship, of course you should do all you can to restore them. But if a leader rebels and, with full consent of his will, defects, then let him defect. If he comes back, then let him start all over again with the process of proving himself.

This militant lack of tolerance couldn't be any plainer than in this line of the hymn they sang. This is not a theological statement; it is a reflection of who they were and how they thought! It says, "If you deny the Lord, the Lord will deny you, too."

From the content of this hymn, it is quite clear that these early saints were extremely serious about their Christianity and the kingdom of God. Their Christian walk wasn't just "another thing" for them to do in life. Christianity was their "all-in-all," and they were giving their lives, lock, stock and barrel, over to this cause.

Please understand, this hymn is not a basis for theology; rather, it is a dramatic reflection of their hour. Church songs are always influenced by preaching, teaching, and prophesying, and they are always indicative of the specific period in which they are written.

The hymn writer, whoever he or she was, chronicled these messages and put them to music so the saints at large could sing them at home, at work, in their leisure time, or at church gatherings.

I can almost hear the first century saints singing the lines of this hymn now! Can you hear them singing?

*"If we are killed like He was killed...*
*Then we shall live again as He now lives eternally...*

*"If suffering is forced upon us...*
*Praise God, we'll reign with Him like nobility...*

*"If we deny or forsake Him...*
*He will deny us of our rewards...*

*"If we believe not, or grow faint-hearted...*
*Still He abideth faithful...*

*"He cannot, cannot, cannot deny — Himself!"*

## The Choice Is Ours To Make

God is doing a new thing for our generation: He is speaking to us in militaristic terms.

He is showing us that we are to be an advancing army upon the dominions of this world.

He is releasing a spirit of WAR inside the Church, and is beckoning us to pick up our knowledge, gifts, and weaponry to use them against the enemy.

The most exciting days of the Church are not behind her; they are *ahead* of her!

In the decades to come, we will see a clash of the kingdoms of this world against the kingdom of God. This clash is even now already beginning to manifest in small ways.

However, as time moves toward the coming of the Lord Jesus Christ, warfare and opposition are going to break out — and we who are listening to God's voice will step forward, prepared to fight it out in the spirit realm with the power of the Holy Ghost.

Are *you* ready for this?

Are *you* flowing with what God is doing?

Are *you* listening? Do *you* hear the voice of our Leader?

Are *you* warring right now like a soldier would?

Are *you* training yourself now to become strong in spirit?

Are *you* being faithful to the task God has given you now?

He is urging us on to wage war!

It is true that the front lines of battle are exciting. But it is also true that this is where satanic attack occurs most frequently. There is no place more exciting or dangerous than the front lines of battle!

*Today — right now — God needs a special brand of believer who will challenge the foe and storm the gates of hell.* He is looking for those special believers who will hear His voice, surrender to His call, and enter and live in the combat zone.

He is calling for those who will step ahead of the rest of the ranks to look the enemy directly in the face; to resist him and drive him back.

Are you one of these? *Are you called to live and fight in the combat zone?*

Are you a real combat zone fighter, or are you simply playing a spiritual "game"? The devil *never* wins a fight, but he *always* wins a "game."

# Other Books by Rick Renner

Dream Thieves
Dressed to Kill
Merchandising the Anointing
Living in the Combat Zone
Seducing Spirits and Doctrines of Demons
Point of No Return
The Dynamic Duo

Additional copies of this book and other book titles from ALBURY PUBLISHING are available at your local bookstore.

Albury Publishing
P. O. Box 470406
Tulsa, Oklahoma 74147-0406

To order tapes by Rick Renner, or to contact him for speaking engagements, please write:

Rick Renner Ministries
P. O. Box 472228
Tulsa, Oklahoma 74147-9994

Unless otherwise indicated, all scriptural quotations are from the *King James Version* of the Bible.

*6th Printing*
*Over 47,000 in Print*

*Living in the Combat Zone*
ISBN 1-88008-902-5
(Formerly ISBN 0-9621436-1-8)

P. O. Box 472228
Tulsa, Oklahoma 74147-9994

Published by Albury Publishing
P. O. Box 470406
Tulsa, Oklahoma 74147-0406

Printed in the United States of America.

# Living in the Combat Zone

*Rick Renner*

ALBURY PUBLISHING